DIRECTIONS

FOR

DAILY COMMUNION WITH GOD,

SHOWING

HOW TO BEGIN, HOW TO SPEND,

AND HOW TO CLOSE

EVERY DAY WITH GOD

BY THE

REV. MATTHEW HENRY

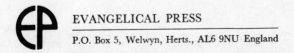
EVANGELICAL PRESS

P.O. Box 5, Welwyn, Herts., AL6 9NU England

Paperback edition issued 1978
by Evangelical Press

from the edition issued in 1848
by Robert Carter

ISBN: 0-85234-112-1

PHOTOLITHOPRINTED BY CUSHING - MALLOY, INC.
ANN ARBOR, MICHIGAN, UNITED STATES OF AMERICA
1978

TO THE READER

THE two first of these Discourses were preached (that is, the substance of them) at the Morning Lecture at Bednal Green, the former, August 13, the other, August 21, 1712. The latter of them I was much importuned to publish by divers that heard it; which yet I had then no thoughts at all of doing, because in divers practical treatises, we have excellent directions given of the same nature and tendency, by better hands than mine. But upon second thoughts I considered, that both those sermons of beginning and spending the day with God, put together, might perhaps be of some use to those into whose hands those larger treatises do not fall. And the truth is, the subject of them is of such a nature, that if they may be of any use, they may be of general and lasting use; whereupon I entertained the thought of writing them over, with very large additions throughout, as God should enable me, for the press. Communicating this thought to some of my friends, they very much encouraged me to proceed in it, but advised me to add a third discourse of closing the day with God, which I thereupon took for my subject at an evening Lecture, September 3, and have likewise much enlarged and altered that. And so this came to be what it is.

I am not without hopes, that something may hereby be contributed among plain people, by the blessing of God upon the endeavor, and the working of his grace with it, to the promoting of serious godliness, which is the thing I aim at. And yet I confess I had not published it, but designing it for a present to my dearly beloved friends in the country, whom I have lately been rent from.

And to them with the most tender affection, and most sincere respects I dedicate it, as a testimony of my abiding concern for their spiritual welfare ; hoping and praying, that their conversation may be in everything as becomes the Gospel of Christ, that whether I come and see them, or else be absent, I may hear comfortably of their affairs, that they stand fast in one spirit with one mind, striving together for the faith of the Gospel.

I am their cordial and affectionate
well wisher,
MATTHEW HENRY

SEPT. 8, 1712

DISCOURSE I

HOW TO BEGIN EVERY DAY WITH GOD

My voice shalt thou hear in the morning, O Lord, in the
morning will I direct my Prayer unto thee, and will look
up.—PSALM v. 3

You would think it a rude question, if I
should ask you, and yet I must entreat you
seriously to ask yourselves, What brings you
hither so early this morning? And what is
your business here? Whenever we are attending on God in holy ordinances (nay, wherever
we are), we should be able to give a good answer to the question which God put to the
prophet. *What dost thou here Elijah?* As
when we return from holy ordinances, we
should be able to give a good answer to the
question which Christ put to those that attended on John Baptist's ministry, *What went
ye out into the wilderness to see?*

It is surprising to see so many got together
here: surely the fields are white unto the harvest; and I am willing to hope, it is not merely for a walk this pleasant morning, that you

are come hither ; or for curiosity, because the
morning lecture was never here before; that
it is not for company, or to meet your friends
here, but that you are come with a pious design to give glory to God, and to receive grace
from him, and in both to keep up your communion with him.   And if you ask us that
are ministers, what our business is, we hope
we can truly say, it is (as God shall enable
us) to assist and further you herein.   Comest
thou peaceably? said the elders of Bethlehem
to Samuel ; and so perhaps you will say to us ;
to which we answer, as the prophet did, peaceably we come to sacrifice unto the Lord, and
invite you to the sacrifice.

While the lecture continues with you, you
have an opportunity of more than doubling
your morning devotions; besides your worshipping of God in secret, and in your families,
which this must not supersede, or jostle out,
you here call upon God's name in the solemn
assembly ; and it is as much your business in
all such exercises to pray a prayer together, as
it is to hear a sermon ; and it is said, the original of the morning exercise was a meeting
for prayer, at the time when the nation was
groaning under the dreadful desolating judgment of a civil war.   You have also an opportunity of conversing with the word of God;
you have precept upon precept, and line upon

line. O that as the opportunity wakens you morning by morning, so (as the prophet speaks) your ears may be wakened to hear as the learned, Isa. l. 4.

But this is not all; we desire that such impressions may be made upon you by this cluster of opportunities, as you may always abide under the influence of; that this morning lecture may leave you better disposed to morning worship ever after; that these frequent acts of devotion may so confirm the habit of it, as that from henceforward your daily worship may become more easy, and if I may so say, in a manner natural to you.

For your help herein I would recommend to you holy David's example in the text, who having resolved in general, *ver.* 2., that he would abound in the duty of prayer, and abide by it, unto thee will I pray, here fixeth one proper time for it, and that is the morning: My voice shalt thou hear in the morning; not in the morning only. David solemnly addressed himself to the duty of prayer three times a day, as Daniel did; Morning and evening, and at noon will I pray, and cry aloud, Psal. lv. 17. Nay, he doth not think that enough, but seven times a day will I praise thee, Psal. cxix. 164 But particularly in the morning.

Doct. It is our wisdom and duty, to begin every day with God.

Let us observe in the text,

1. The good work itself that we are to do. God must hear our voice, we must direct our prayer to him, and we must look up.

2. The special time appointed, and observed for the doing of this good work ; and that is in the morning, and again in the morning, that is, every morning, as duly as the morning comes.

For the first, The good work which by the example of David we are here taught to do, is in one word to pray ; a duty dictated by the light and law of nature, which plainly and loudly speaks, Should not a people seek unto their God ? But which the Gospel of Christ gives us much better instructions in, and encouragement to, than any that nature furnisheth us with, for it tells us what we must pray for, in whose name we must pray, and by whose assistance, and invites us to come boldly to the throne of grace, and to enter into the holiest by the blood of Jesus. This work we are to do not on the morning only, but at other times, at all times ; we read of preaching the word out of season, but we do not read of praying out of season, for that is never out of season ; the throne of grace is always open, and humble supplicants are always welcome, and cannot come unseasonably.

But let us see how David here expresseth his pious resolution to abide by this duty.

1. *My voice shalt thou hear.* Two ways David may here be understood. Either,

1. *As promising himself a gracious acceptance with God.* Thou shalt, *i. e.* thou wilt hear my voice, when in the morning I direct my prayer to thee ; so it is the language of his faith, grounded upon God's promise, that his ear shall be always open to his people's cry. He had prayed, *ver.* 1. Give ear to my words, O Lord ; and *ver.* 2. Hearken unto the voice of my cry ; and here he receives an answer to that prayer, thou wilt hear, I doubt not but thou wilt ; and though I have not presently a grant of the thing I prayed for, yet I am sure my prayer is heard, is accepted, and comes up for a memorial, as the prayer of Cornelius did ; it is put upon the file, and shall not be forgotten. If we look inward, and can say by experience that God has prepared our heart ; we may look upward, may look forward, and say with confidence that he will cause his ear to hear.

We may be sure of this, and we must pray in the assurance of it, in a full assurance of his faith, that wherever God finds a praying heart, he will be found a prayer-hearing God ;

though the voice of prayer be a low voice, a weak voice, yet if it come from an upright heart, it is a voice that God will hear, that he will hear with pleasure, it is his delight, and that he will return a gracious answer to; he hath heard thy prayers, he hath seen thy tears. When therefore we stand praying, this ground we must stand upon, this principle we must stand to, nothing doubting, nothing wavering, that whatever we ask of God as a father, in the name of Jesus Christ the Mediator, according to the will of God revealed in the scripture, it shall be granted us either in kind or kindness; so the promise is, John xvi. 23.; and the truth of it is sealed to by the concurring experience of the saints in all ages, ever since men began to call upon the name of the Lord, that Jacob's God never yet said to Jacob's seed, seek ye me in vain, and he will not begin now. When we come to God by prayer, if we come aright we may be confident of this, that notwithstanding the distance between heaven and earth, and our great unworthiness to have any notice taken of us, or any favor showed us; yet God doth hear our voice, and will not turn away our prayer, or his mercy. Or,

2. It is rather to be taken, as David's promising God a constant attendance on him, in the way he has appointed. My voice shalt

thou hear, *i. e.* I will speak to thee; because thou hast inclined thine ear unto me many a time, therefore I have taken up a resolution to call upon thee at all times, even to the end of my time. Not a day shall pass, but thou shalt be sure to hear from me. Not that the voice is the thing that God regards, as they seemed to think, who in prayer made their voice to be heard on high, Isa. lviii. 4. Hannah prayed and prevailed, when her voice was not heard; but it is the voice of the heart that is here meant; God saith to Moses, wherefore criest thou unto me, when we do not find that he said one word, Exod. xiv. 15. Praying is lifting up the soul to God, and pouring out the heart before him; yet as far as the expressing of the devout affections of the heart by words may be of use to fix the thoughts, and to excite and quicken the desires, it is good to draw near to God, not only with a pure heart, but with a humble voice; so must we render the calves of our lips.

However, God understands the language of the heart, and that is the language in which we must speak to God; David prays here, *ver*. 1. not only give ear to my words, but consider my meditation, and Psal. xix. 14. Let the words of my mouth, proceeding from the meditation of my heart, be acceptable in thy sight.

This therefore we have to do in every prayer, we must speak to God; we must write to him; we say we hear from a friend whom we receive a letter from; we must see to it that God hears from us daily.

1. He expects and requires it. Though he has no need of us or our services, nor can be benefited by them, yet he has obliged us to offer the sacrifice of prayer and praise to him continually.

(1.) Thus he will keep up his authority over us, and keep us continually in mind of our subjection to him, which we are apt to forget. He requires that by prayer we solemnly pay our homage to him, and give honor to his name, that by this act and deed of our own, thus frequently repeated, we may strengthen the obligations we lie under toobserve his statutes and keep his laws, and be more and more sensible of the weight of them. He is thy Lord, and worship thou him, that by frequent humble adorations of his perfections, thou mayest make a constant humble compliance with his will the more easy to thee. By doing obeisance we are learning obedience.

(2.) Thus he will testify his love and compassion towards us. It would have been an abundant evidence of his concern for us, and his goodness to us, if he had only said, let me hear from you as often as there is occasion;

call upon me in the time of trouble or want, and that is enough ; but to show his complacency in us, as a father doth his affection to his child when he is sending him abroad, he gives us this charge, Let me hear from you every day, by every post, though you have no particular business; which shows, that the prayer of the upright is his delight ; it is music in his ears ; Christ saith to his dove, Let me see thy countenance, let me hear thy voice, for sweet is thy voice, and thy countenance is comely, Cant. ii. 14. And it is to the spouse the church that Christ speaks in the close of that Song of Songs, O thou that dwellest in the gardens, (in the original it is feminine) the companions hearken to thy voice, cause me to hear it. What a shame is this to us, that God is more willing to be prayed to, and more ready to hear prayer than we are to pray.

2. We have something to say to God every day. Many are not sensible of this, and it is their sin and misery ; they live without God in the world, they think they can live without him, are not sensible of their dependence upon him, and their obligations to him, and therefore for their parts they have nothing to say to him ; he never hears from them, no more than the father did from his prodigal son, when he was upon the ramble, from one week's end to another. They ask scornfully, what can the

Almighty do for them? and then no marvel
if they ask next, what profit shall we have if
we pray unto him? And the result is, they
say to the Almighty, depart from us, and so
shall their doom be. But I hope better things
of you my brethren, and that you are not of
those who cast off fear, and restrain prayer before God; you are all ready to own that there
is a great deal that the Almighty can do for
you, and that there is profit in praying to him,
and therefore resolve to draw nigh to God, that
he may draw nigh to you.

We have something to say to God daily.

(1.) As to a friend we love and have freedom with; such a friend we cannot go by
without calling on, and never want something
to say to, though we have no particular business with him; to such a friend we unbosom
ourselves, we profess our love and esteem, and
with pleasure communicate our thoughts;
Abraham is called the friend of God, and this
honor have all the saints, I have not called you
servants, (saith Christ,) but friends; his secret
is with the righteous; we are invited to ac-
quaint ourselves with him, and to walk with
him as one friend walks with another; the
fellowship of believers is said to be with the
Father, and with his Son Jesus Christ; and
have we nothing to say to him then?

Is it not errand enough to the throne of his

grace to admire his infinite perfections, which we can never fully comprehend, and yet never sufficiently contemplate, and take complacency in? To please ourselves in beholding the beauty of the Lord, and giving him the glory due to his name? Have we not a great deal to say to him in acknowledgment of his condescending grace and favor to us, in manifesting himself to us and not to the world: and in profession of our affection and submission to him; Lord, thou knowest all things, thou knowest that I love thee.

God hath something to say to us as a friend every day, by the written word, in which we must hear his voice, by his providences, and by our own consciences, and he hearkens and hears whether we have anything to say to him by way of reply, and we are very unfriendly if we have not. When he saith to us, Seek ye my face, should not our hearts answer as to one we love, Thy face, Lord, will we seek. When he saith to us, Return ye backsliding children, should not we readily reply, Behold we come unto thee, for thou art the Lord our God. If he speak to us by way of conviction and reproof, ought not we to return an answer by way of confession and submission? If he speak to us by way of comfort, ought not we to reply in praise? If you love God, you cannot be to seek for something to say to him, something for your hearts to pour out before him, which his grace has already put there.

(2.) As to a master we serve, and have business with. Think how numerous and important the concerns are that lie between us and God, and you will readily acknowledge that you have a great deal to say to him. We have a constant dependence upon him, all our expectation is from him; we have constant dealings with him; he is the God with whom we have to do, Heb. iv. 13.

Do we not know that our happiness is bound up in his favor; it is life, the life of our souls, it is better than life, than the life of our bodies? And have we not business with God to seek his favor, to entreat it with our whole hearts, to beg as for our lives that he would lift up the light of his countenance upon us, and to plead Christ's righteousness, as that only through which we can hope to obtain God's loving kindness?

Do we not know that we have offended God, that by sin we have made ourselves obnoxious to his wrath and curse, and that we are daily contracting guilt? And have we not then business enough with him to confess our fault and folly, to ask for pardon in the blood of Christ, and in him who is our peace to make our peace with God, and renew our covenants with him in his own strength to go and sin no more?

Do we not know that we have daily work to do for God, and our own souls, the work of the day that is to be done in its day? And have we not then business with God to beg of him to show us what he would have us do, to direct us in it, and strengthen us for it? To seek to him for assistance and acceptance, that he will work in us both to will and to do that which is good, and then countenance and own his own work? Such business as this the servant has with his master.

Do we not know that we are continually in danger? Our bodies are so, and their lives and comforts? we are continually surrounded with diseases and deaths, whose arrows fly at midnight and at noonday; and have we not then business with God going out and coming in, lying down and rising up, to put ourselves under the protections of his providence, to be the charge of his holy angels? Our souls much more are so, and their lives and comforts; it is those our adversary the devil, a strong and subtle adversary, wars against, and seeks to devour; and have we not then business with God to put ourselves under the protection of his grace, and clothe ourselves with his armor, that we may be able to stand against the wiles and violences of Satan; so as we may neither be surprised into sin by a sudden temptation, nor overpowered by a strong one?

Do we not know that we are dying daily, that death is working in us, and hastening towards us, and that death fetches us to judgment, and judgment fixeth us in our everlasting state? And have we not then something to say to God in preparation for what is before us? Shall we not say, Lord make us to know our end! Lord teach us to number our days! Have we not business with God to judge ourselves that we may not be judged, and to see that our matters be right and good?

Do we not know that we are members of that body whereof Christ is the head, and are we not concerned to approve ourselves living members? Have we not then business with God upon the public account to make intercession for his church? Have we nothing to say for Zion? Nothing in behalf of Jerusalem's ruined walls? Nothing for the peace and welfare of the land of our nativity? Are we not of the family, or but babes in it, that we concern not ourselves in the concerns of it.

Have we no relations, no friends, that are dear to us, whose joys and griefs we share in? And have we nothing to say to God for them? No complaints to make, no requests to make known? Are none of them sick or in distress?

None of them tempted or disconsolate? And have we not errands at the throne of grace, to beg relief and succor for them?

Now lay all this together, and then consider whether you have not something to say to God every day; and particularly in days of trouble, when it is meet to be said unto God, I have borne chastisement; and when if you have any sense of things, you will say unto God, do not condemn me.

3. If you have all this to say to God, what should hinder you from saying it? from saying it every day? Why should not he hear your voice, when you have so many errands to him?

1. Let not distance hinder you from saying it. You have occasion to speak with a friend, but he is a great way off, you cannot reach him, you know not where to find him, nor how to get a letter to him, and therefore your business with him is undone; but this needs not keep you from speaking to God, for though it is true God is in heaven, and we are upon earth, yet he is nigh to his praying people in all that they call upon him for, he hears their voice wherever they are. Out of the depths I have cried unto thee, saith David, Psal. cxxx. 1. From the ends of the earth I will cry unto thee, Psal. lxi. 2. Nay, Jonah saith, Out of the belly of hell cried I, and thou heardest my

voice. In all places we may find a way open
heavenward; *Undique ad Cœlos tantundem
est Viæ;* Thanks to him who by his own
blood has consecrated for us a new and living
way into the holiest, and settled a correspond-
ence between heaven and earth.

2. Let not fear hinder you from saying
what you have to say to God. You have
business with a great man it may be, but he
is far above you, or so stern and severe towards
all his inferiors, that you are afraid to speak to
him, and you have none to introduce you, or
speak a good word for you, and therefore you
choose rather to drop your cause; but there is
no occasion for your being thus discouraged in
speaking to God; you may come boldly to the
throne of his grace, you have there a PARRHE-
SIA, *a liberty of speech*, leave to pour out your
whole souls. And such are his compassions to
humble supplicants, that even his terror need
not make them afraid. It is against the mind
of God that you should frighten yourselves, he
would have you encourage yourselves, for you
have not received the spirit of bondage again
to fear, but the spirit of adoption, by which you
are brought into this among other the glorious
liberties of the children of God. Nor is this
all, we have one to introduce us, and to speak
for us, an advocate with the Father. Did ever
children need an advocate with a father? But

that by those two immutable things in which
it is impossible for God to lie, we might have
strong consolation, we have not only the relation of a father to depend upon, but the interest and intercession of an advocate; a High
Priest over the house of God, in whose name
we have access with confidence.

3. Let not his knowing what your business
is, and what you have to say to him hinder
you, you have business with such a friend, but
you think you need not put yourselves to any
trouble about it, for he is already apprized of
it; he knows what you want and what you
desire, and therefore it is no matter for speaking to him, it is true all your desire is before
God, he knows your wants and burthens, but
he will know them from you; he hath promised you relief; but his promise must be
put in suit, and he will for this be inquired of
by the house of Israel to do it for them, Ezek.
xxxvi. 37. Though we cannot by our prayers
give him any information, yet we must by our
prayers give him honor. It is true, nothing
we can say can have any influence upon him,
or move him to show us mercy, but it may
have an influence upon ourselves, and help to
put us into a frame fit to receive mercy. It is
a very easy and reasonable condition of his
favors, Ask, and it shall be given you. It was
to teach us the necessity of praying, in order

to our receiving favor, that Christ put that strange question to the blind men, What would ye that I should do unto you? He knew what they would have, but those that touch the top of the golden sceptre must be ready to tell, what is their petition and what is their request?

4. Let not any other business hinder our saying what we have to say to God. We have business with a friend perhaps, but we cannot do it, because we have not leisure ; we have something else to do, which we think more needful; but we cannot say so concerning the business we have to do with God ; for that is without doubt the one thing needful, to which everything else must be made to truckle and give way. It is not at all necessary to our happiness that we be great in the world, or raise estates to such a pitch. But it is absolutely necessary that we make our peace with God, that we obtain his favor, and keep ourselves with his love. Therefore no business for the world will serve to excuse our attendance upon God, but on the contrary, the more important our worldly business is, the more need we have to apply ourselves to God by prayer for his blessing upon it, and so take him along with us in it. The closer we keep to prayer, and to God in prayer, the more will all our affairs prosper.

Shall I prevail with you now to let God frequently hear from you; let him hear your voice, though it be but the voice of your breathing, (Lam. iii. 56.) that is a sign of life; though it be the voice of your groanings, and those so weak that they cannot be uttered, Rom. viii. 26. Speak to him, though it be in broken language, as Hezekiah did; *Like a crane or a swallow, so did I chatter,* Isa. xxxviii. 14. Speak often to him, he is always within hearing. Hear him speaking to you, and have an eye to that in everything you say to him: as when you write an answer to a letter of business, you lay it before you; God's word must be the guide of your desires, and the ground of your expectations in prayer, nor can you expect he should give a gracious ear to what you say to him, if you turn a deaf ear to what he saith to you.

You see you have frequent occasion to speak with God, and therefore are concerned to grow in your acquaintance with him, to take heed of doing anything to displease him; and to strengthen your interest in the Lord Jesus, through whom alone it is that you have access with boldness to him. Keep your voice in tune for prayer, and let all your language be a pure language, that you may be fit to call on the name of the Lord, Zeph. iii. 9. And in every prayer remember you are speaking to

God, and make it to appear you have an awe
of him upon your spirits ; let us not be rash
with our mouth, nor hasty to utter anything
before God, but let every word be well weigh-
ed because God is in heaven, and we upon
earth, Eccl. v. 2.   And if he had not invited
and encouraged us to do it, it had been unpar-
donable presumption for such sinful worms as
we are to speak to the Lord of glory, Gen.
xviii. 27.   And we are concerned to speak from
the heart heartily, for it is for our lives and for
the lives of our souls that we are speaking to
him.

2. We must direct our prayer unto God.
He must not only hear our voice, but we must
with deliberation and design address ourselves
to him.   In the original it is no more but I will
direct unto thee ; it might be supplied, I will
direct my soul unto thee, agreeing with Psal.
xxv. 1.   Unto thee, O Lord, do I lift up my
soul.   Or, I will direct my affections to thee ;
having set my love upon thee, I will let out
my love to thee.   Our translation supplies it
very well, I will direct my prayer unto thee.
That is,

1. When I pray to thee I will direct my
prayers ; and then it notes a fixedness of
thoughts, and a close application of mind, to
the duty of prayer.   We must go about it
solemnly, as those that have something of mo-

ment much at heart, and much in view therein, and therefore dare not trifle in it. When
we go to pray, we must not give the sacrifice
of fools, that think not either what is to be
done, or what is to be gained, but speak the
words of the wise, who aim at some good end
in what they say, and suit it to that end, we
must have in our eye God's glory and our own
true happiness; and so well ordered is the
covenant of grace, that God has been pleased
therein to twist interests with us, so that in
seeking his glory, we really and effectually
seek our own true interests. This is directing
the prayer, as he that shoots an arrow at a
mark directs it, and with a fixed eye and
steady hand takes aim aright. This is en-
gaging the heart to approach to God, and in
order to that disengaging it from everything
else. He that takes aim with one eye shuts
the other; if we would direct a prayer to God,
we must look off all other things, must gather
in our wandering thoughts, must summon
them all to draw near and give their attendance, for here is work to be done that needs
them all, and is well worthy of them all; thus
we must be able to say with the psalmist, O
God, my heart is fixed, my heart is fixed.

2. When I direct my prayer, I will direct it
to thee. And so it speaks,

1. The sincerity of our habitual intention

in prayer. We must not direct our prayer to men, that we may gain praise and applause with them, as the Pharisees did, who proclaimed their devotions as they did their alms, that they might gain a reputation, which they knew how to make a hand of; Verily they have their reward, men commend them, but God abhors their pride and hypocrisy. We must not let our prayers run at large, as they did that said, Who will show us any good? Nor direct them to the world, courting its smiles, and pursuing its wealth, as those that are therefore said not to cry unto God with their hearts, because they assembled themselves for corn and wine, Hos. vii. 14. Let not self, carnal self, be the spring and centre of your prayers, but God; let the eye of the soul be fixed upon him as your highest end in your applications to him; let this be the habitual disposition of your souls, to be to your God for a name and a praise; and let this be your design in all your desires, that God may be glorified, and by this let them all be directed, determined, sanctified, and when need is overruled. Our Saviour hath plainly taught us this, in the first petition of the Lord's prayer; which is, hallowed be thy name: In that we fix our end, and other things are desired in order to that; in that the prayer is directed to the glory of God, in all that whereby he has made himself known, the glory of his holiness, and it is with an eye to the sanctifying of his name, that we desire his kingdom may come, and his will be done, and that we may be fed, and kept, and pardoned. An habitual aim at God's glory is that sincerity which is our Gospel-perfection. That single eye, which, where it is, the whole body, the whole soul is full of light. Thus the prayer is directed to God.

2. It speaks the steadiness of our actual regard to God in prayer. We must direct our prayer to God, that is, we must continually think of him, as one with whom we have to do in prayer. We must direct our prayer, as we direct our speech to the person we have business with. The Bible is a letter God hath sent to us, prayer is a letter we send to him; now you know it is essential to a letter that it be directed, and material that it be directed right; if it be not, it is in danger of miscarrying; which may be of ill consequence; you pray daily, and therein send letters to God; you know not what you lose, if your letters miscarry; will you therefore take instructions how to direct to him?

1. Give him his titles as you do when you direct to a person of honor; address yourselves to him as the great Jehovah, God over all, blessed for evermore; the King of kings, and Lord of lords: as the Lord God gracious and

merciful; let your hearts and mouths be filled with holy adorings and admirings of him, and fasten upon those titles of his, which are proper to strike a holy awe of him upon your minds, that you may worship him with reverence and godly fear. Direct your prayer to him as the God of glory, with whom is terrible majesty, and whose greatness is unsearchable, that you may not dare to trifle with him, or to mock him in what you say to him.

2. Take notice of your relation to him, as his children, and let not that be overlooked and lost in your awful adorations of his glories. I have been told of a good man, among whose experiences, which he kept a record of, after his death, this among other things was found: that such a time in secret prayer, his heart at the beginning of the duty was much enlarged in giving to God those titles which are awful and tremendous, in calling him the Great, the Mighty, and the Terrible God, but going on thus, he checked himself with this thought, and why not my Father? Christ hath both by his precept and by his pattern, taught us to address ourselves to God as our Father? and the spirit of adoption teacheth us to cry, Abba, Father; a son, though a prodigal, when he returns and repents, may go to his father, and say unto him, Father, I have sinned; and though no more worthy to be called a son, yet

humbly bold to call him father. When
Ephraim bemoans himself as a bullock unac-
customed to the yoke, God bemoans him as a
dear son, as a pleasant child, Jer. xxxi. 18, 20,
and if God is not ashamed, let us not be afraid
to own the relation.

3. Direct your prayer to him in heaven;
this our Saviour has taught us in the preface
to the Lord's prayer, Our Father which art in
heaven. Not that he is confined to the heavens, or as if the heaven, or heaven of heavens
could contain him, but there he is said to have
prepared his throne, not only his throne of government by which his kingdom ruleth over all,
but his throne of grace to which we must by
faith draw near. We must eye him as God in
heaven, in opposition to the god of the heathen,
which dwelt in temples made with hands.
Heaven is a high place, and we must address
ourselves to him as a God infinitely above us;
it is the fountain of light, and to him we must
address ourselves as the Father of lights; it is
a place of prospect, and we must see his eye
upon us, from thence beholding all the children
of men ; it is a place of purity, and we must in
prayer eye him as an holy God, and give thanks
at the remembrance of his holiness; it is the
firmament of his power, and we must depend
upon him as one to whom power belongs.
When our Lord Jesus prayed, he lift up his

eyes to heaven, to direct us whence to expect the blessings we need.

4. Direct this letter to be left with the Lord Jesus, the only Mediator between God and man ; it will certainly miscarry if it be not put into his hand, who is that other angel that puts much incense to the prayers of the saints, and so perfumed presents them to the Father, Rev. viii. 3. What we ask of the Father must be in his name; what we expect from the Father must be by his hand, for he is the High Priest of our profession, that is ordained for men to offer their gifts; Heb. v. 1. Direct the letter to be left with him, and he will deliver it with care and speed, and will make our service acceptable. Mr. George Herbert, in his poem called the Bag, having pathetically described the wound in Christ's side as he was hanging on the cross, makes him speak thus to all believers as he was going to heaven.

> If you have anything to send or write,
>   I have no bag, but here is room,
> Unto my Father's hands and sight,
>   Believe me it shall safely come;
> That I shall mind what you impart,
>   Look, you may put it very near my hear
> Or, if hereafter any of my friends
>   Will use me in this kind, the door
> Shall still be open, what he sends
>   I will present, and something more,
> Not to his hurt; sighs will convey
>   Anything to me; hark, despair, away.

3. We must look up, that is,

1. We must look up in our prayers, as those that speak to one above us, infinitely above us, the high and holy One that inhabiteth eternity, as those that expect every good and perfect gift to come from above, from the Father of lights; as those that desire in prayer to enter into the holiest, and to draw near with a true heart. With an eye of faith we must look above the world and everything in it, must look beyond the things of time; what is this world, and all things here below, to one that knows how to put a due estimate upon spiritual blessings in heavenly things by Jesus Christ? The spirit of a man at death goes upward; (Eccl. iii. 21.,) for it returns to God who gave it, and therefore as mindful of its original, it must in every prayer look upwards, towards its God, towards its home, as having set its affections on things above, wherein it has laid up its treasure. Let us therefore in prayer lift up our hearts with our hands unto God in the heavens. Lam. iii. 14. It was anciently usual in some churches for the minister to stir up the people to pray with this word, Sursum Corda, up with your hearts; unto thee, O Lord, do we lift up our souls.

2. We must look up after our prayers.

1. With an eye of satisfaction and pleasure; looking up is a sign of cheerfulness, as a down

look is a melancholy one. We must look up
as those that having by prayer referred ourselves to God, are easy and well pleased, and
with an entire confidence in his wisdom and
goodness patiently expect the issue. Hannah,
when she had prayed, looked up, looked pleasant ; she went her way, and did eat, and her
countenance was no more sad, 1 Sam. i. 18.
Prayer is heart's ease to a good Christian ; and
when we have prayed, we should look up as
those that through grace have found it so.

2. With an eye of observation, what returns
God makes to our prayers. We must look up
as one that has shot an arrow looks after it to
see how near it comes to the mark ; we must
look within us, and observe what the frame of
our spirit is after we have been at prayer, how
well satisfied they are in the will of God, and
how well disposed to accommodate themselves
to it ; we must look about us, and observe how
Providence works concerning us, that if our
prayers be answered, we may return to give
thanks ; if not, we may remove what hinders,
and may continue waiting. Thus we must
set ourselves upon our watch-tower to see what
God will say unto us, Heb. ii. 1, and must be
ready to hear it, Psal. lxxxv. 8, expecting that
God will give us an answer of peace, and resolving that we will return no more to folly.
Thus must we keep up our communion with

God; hoping that whenever we lift up our hearts unto him, he will lift up the light of his countenance upon us. Sometimes the answer is quick, while they are yet speaking I will hear; quicker than the return of any of your posts, but if it be not, when we have prayed we must wait.

Let us learn thus to direct our prayers, and thus to look up; to be inward with God in every duty, to make heart-work of it, or we make nothing of it. Let us not worship in the outward court, when we are commanded and encouraged to enter within the veil.

For the Second. The particular time fixed in the text for this good work, is the morning; and the Psalmist seems to lay an emphasis upon this, in the morning, and again, in the morning; not then only, but then to begin with : Let that be one of the hours of prayer. Under the law, we find that every morning there was a lamb offered in sacrifice, Exod. xxix. 39, and every morning the priest burned incense, Exod. xxx. 7, and the singers stood every morning to thank the Lord, 1. Chron. xxiii. 10. And so it was appointed in Ezekiel's temple, Ezek. xlvi. 13, 14, 15. By which an intimation was plainly given, that the spiritual sacrifices should be offered by the spiritual priests every morning, as duly as the morning comes. Every Christian should pray in secret,

and every master of a family with his family
morning by morning; and there is good reason
for it.

1. The morning is the first part of the day,
and it is fit that he that is the first should have
the first, and be first served. The heathen
could say, *A Jove Principium*, whatever you
do begin with God. The world had its beginning from him, we had ours, and therefore
whatever we begin, it concerns us to take him
along with us in it. The days of our life, as
soon as ever the sun of reason riseth in the
soul, should be devoted to God, and employed
in his service; from the womb of the morning,
let Christ have the dew of the youth, Psal. cx.
3. The first-fruits were always to be the
Lord's, and the firstlings of the flock. By
morning and evening prayer we give glory to
him who is the Alpha and the Omega, the
first and the last; with him we must begin
and end the day, begin and end the night, who
is the beginning and the end, the first cause,
and the last end.

Wisdom hath said, Those that seek me
early shall find me; early in their lives, early
in the day; for hereby we give to God that
which he ought to have, the preference above
other things. Hereby we show that we are in
care to please him, and to approve ourselves to
him, and that we seek him diligently. What

we do earnestly, we are said in scripture to do early, (as Psal. ci. 8.) Industrious men rise betimes; David expresseth the strength and warmth of his devotion, when he saith, O God thou art my God, early will I seek thee, Psal. lxiii. 1.

2. In the morning we are fresh and living, and in the best frame. When our spirits are revived with the rest and sleep of the night, and we live a kind of new life; and the fatigues of the day before are forgotten; the God of Israel neither slumbers nor sleeps, yet when he exerts himself more than ordinary on his people's behalf, he is said to awake as one out of sleep, Psal. lxxviii. 65. If ever we be good for anything, it is in the morning, it is therefore become a Proverb, *Aurora Musis Amica;* and if the morning be a friend to the muses, I am sure it is no less so to the graces. As he that is the first should have the first; so he that is the best should have the best; and then when we are fittest for business, we should apply ourselves to that which is the most needful business.

Worshipping God is work that requires the best powers of the soul, when they are at the best; and it well deserves them; how can they be better bestowed, or so as to turn to a better account? Let all that is within me bless his holy name, saith David, and all little

enough. If there be any gift in us by which
God may be honored, the morning is the most
proper time to stir it up, (2 Tim. i. 6.,) when
our spirits are refreshed, and have gained new
vigor ; then awake my Glory, awake psaltery
and harp, for I myself will awake early, Psal.
lvii. 8. Then let us stir up ourselves to take
hold on God.

3. In the morning we are most free from
company and business, and ordinarily have the
best opportunity for solitude and retirement; unless we be of those sluggards that lie in bed
with yet a little sleep, a little slumber, till the
work of their calling calls them up, with how
long wilt thou sleep, O sluggard ? It is the
wisdom of those that have much to do in the
world, that have scarce a minute to themselves
of all day, to take time in the morning before
business crowds in upon them, for the business
of their religion ; that they may be entire for
it, and therefore the more intent upon it.

As we are concerned to worship God, then
when we are least burthened with deadness
and dulness within, so also when we are least
exposed to distraction and diversion from without ; the apostle intimates how much it should
be our care to attend upon the Lord without
distraction, 1 Cor. vii. 35. And therefore that
one day in seven, (and it is the first day too,
the morning of the week,) which is appointed

for holy work, is appointed to be a day of rest
from other work. Abraham leaves all at the
bottom of the hill, when he goes up into the
mount to worship God. In the morning therefore let us converse with God, and apply ourselves to the concerns of the other life, before
we are entangled in the affairs of this life.
Our Lord Jesus has set us an example of this,
who because his day was wholly filled up with
public business for God and the souls of men,
rose up in the morning a great while before
day, and before company came in, and went
out into a solitary place, and there prayed,
Mark i. 35.

4. In the morning we have received fresh
mercies from God, which we are concerned to
acknowledge with thankfulness to his praise.
He is continually doing us good, and loading
us with his benefits. Every day we have reason to bless him, for every day he is blessing
us ; in the morning particularly ; and therefore
as he is giving out to us the fruits of his favor,
which are said to be new every morning, Lam.
iii. 23, because though the same that we had
the morning before, they are still forfeited, and
still needed, and upon that account may be
called still new ; so we should be still returning the expressions of our gratitude to him,
and of other pious and devout affections, which

like the fire on the altar, must be new every morning, Lev. vi. 12.

Have we had a good night, and have we not an errand to the throne of grace to return thanks for it? How many mercies concurred to make it a good night? Distinguishing mercies granted to us, but denied to others; many have not where to lay their heads; our master himself had not; the foxes have holes, and the birds of the air have nests, but the Son of Man hath not where to lay his head; but we have houses to dwell in, quiet and peaceable habitations, perhaps stately ones : We have beds to lie in, warm and easy ones, perhaps beds of ivory, fine ones, such as they stretched themselves upon that were at ease in Zion ; and are not put to wander in deserts and mountains, in dens and caves of the earth, as some of the best of God's saints have been forced to do, of whom the world was not worthy. Many have beds to lie on, yet dare not, or cannot lie down in them, being kept up either by the sickness of their friends, or the fear of their enemies. But we have laid us down, and there have been none to make us afraid; no alarms of the sword, either of war or persecution. Many lay them down and cannot sleep, but are full of tossings to and fro until the dawning of the day, through pain of body, or anguish of mind. Wearisome nights are ap-

pointed to them, and their eyes are held
waking : but we have laid us down and slept
without any disturbance, and our sleep was
sweet and refreshing, the pleasant parenthesis
of our cares and toils ; it is God that has given
us sleep, has given it us as he gives it to his
beloved.   Many lay them down and sleep, and
never rise again, they sleep the sleep of death,
and their beds are their graves ; but we have
slept and waked again, have rested, and are
refreshed ; we shake ourselves, and it is with
us as at other times ; because the Lord hath
sustained us ; and if he had not upheld us, we
had sunk with our own weight when we fell
asleep, Psal. iii. 5.

Have we a pleasant morning ?   Is the light
sweet to us, the light of the sun, the light of
the eyes, do these rejoice the heart ?   And
ought not we to own our obligations to him
who opens our eyes, and opens the eyelids of
the morning upon us ?   Have we clothes to
put on in the morning, garments that are warm
upon us, Job xxxvii. 17.   Change of raiment,
not for necessity only, but for ornament ?   We
have them from God, it is his wool and his
flax, that is given to cover our nakedness, and
the morning when we dress ourselves, is the
proper time of returning him thanks for it ; yet
I doubt we do it not so constantly as we do for
our food when we sit down to our tables,

though we have as much reason to do it. Are we in health and at ease? Have we been long so? We ought to be as thankful for a constant series of mercies, as for particular instances of it, especially considering how many are sick and in pain, and how much we have deserved to be so.

Perhaps we have experienced some special mercy to ourselves or our families, in preservation from fire or thieves, from dangers we have been aware of, and many more unseen; weeping perhaps endured for a night, and joy came in the morning, and that calls aloud upon us to own the goodness of God. The destroying angel perhaps has been abroad, and the arrow that flies at midnight, and wasteth in darkness, has been shot in at others' windows, but our houses have been passed over, thanks be to God for the blood of the covenant sprinkled upon our door-posts; and for the ministration of the good angels about, to which we owe it, that we have been preserved from the malice of the evil angels against us, those rulers of the darkness of this world who perhaps creep forth like the beasts of prey, when he maketh darkness and it is dark. All the glory be to the God of the angels.

5. In the morning we have fresh matter ministered to us for adoration of the greatness and glory of God. We ought to take notice

not only of the gifts of God's bounty to us,
which we have the comfort and benefit of, they
are little narrow souls that confine their regards to them; but we ought to observe the
more general instances of his wisdom and
power in the kingdom of providence which re-
dound to his honor, and the common good of
the universe. The 19th psalm seems to have
been a *Morning Meditation*, in which we are
directed to observe how the heavens declare the
glory of God, and the firmament showeth his
handy-work; and to own not only the advantage we receive from their light and influence,
but the honor they do to him who stretched
out the heavens like a curtain, fixed their pil-
lars, and established their ordinances, according to which they continue to this day, for
they are all his servants. Day by day utters
this speech, and night unto night showeth this
knowledge, even the eternal power and God-
head of the great Creator of the world, and its
great ruler. The regular and constant suc-
cession and revolution of light and darkness,
according to the original contract made between them, that they should reign alternately,
may serve to confirm our faith, in that part of
divine Revelation which gives us the history
of the creation, and the promise of God to Noah
and his sons, Gen. viii. 22. His covenant with
the day and with the night, Jer. xxxiii. 20.

Look up in the morning, and see how exactly the dayspring knows its place, knows its time, and keeps them, how the morning light takes hold of the ends of the earth, and of the air, which is turned to it as clay to the seal' instantly receiving the impressions of it, Job xxviii. 12, 13, 14. I was pleased with an expression of a worthy good minister I heard lately, in his thanksgivings to God for the mercies of the morning; How many thousand miles (said he) has the sun travelled this last night to bring the light of the morning to us poor sinful wretches, that justly might have been buried in the darkness of the night. Look up, and see the sun as a bridegroom richly dressed, and hugely pleased, coming out of his chamber, and rejoicing as a strong man to run a race ; observe how bright his beams are, how sweet his smiles, how strong his influences : And if there be no speech or language where their voice is not heard, the voice of these natural immortal preachers, proclaiming the glory of God, it is pity there should be any speech or language where the voice of his worshippers should not be heard, echoing to the voice of those preachers, and ascribing glory to him who thus makes the morning and evening to rejoice : But whatever others do, let him hear our voice to this purpose in the morn-

ing, and in the morning let us direct our praise
unto him.

6. In the morning we have, or should have
had fresh thoughts of God, and sweet meditations on his name, and those we ought to offer
up to him in prayer. Have we been, according to David's example, remembering God upon
our beds, and meditating upon him in the night
watches ? When we awake, can we say, as
he did, we are still with God ? If so, we have
a good errand to the throne of grace by the
words of our mouths, to offer up to God the
meditations of our hearts, and it will be to him
a sacrifice of a sweet smelling savor. If the
heart has been inditing a good matter, let the
tongue be as the pen of a ready writer, to pour
it out before God, Psal. xlv. 1.

We have the word of God to converse with,
and we ought to read a portion of it every
morning : By it God speaks to us, and in it we
ought to meditate day and night, which if we
do, that will send us to the throne of grace, and
furnish us with many a good errand there. If
God in the morning by his grace direct his
word to us, so as to make it reach our hearts,
that will engage us to direct our prayer to him.

7. In the morning, it is to be feared, we find
cause to reflect on many vain and sinful thoughts
that have been in our minds in the night season ; and, upon that account, it is necessary we

address ourselves to God by prayer in the morning, for the pardon of them. The Lord's prayer seems to be calculated primarily in the letter of it for the morning; for we are taught to pray for our daily bread this day: And yet we are then to pray, Father, forgive us our trespasses; for, as in the hurry of the day we contract guilt by our irregular words and actions, so we do in the solitude of the night, by our corrupt imaginations, and the wanderings of an unsanctified, ungoverned fancy. It is certain, the thought of foolishness is sin, Prov. xxiv. 9. Foolish thoughts are sinful thoughts; the first-born of the old man, the first beginnings of all sin; and how many of these vain thoughts lodge within us wherever we lodge; their name is legion, for they are many: Who can understand these errors! They are more than the hairs of our head. We read of those that work evil upon their beds, because there they devise it; and when the morning is light they practise it, Mic. ii. 1. How often in the night season is the mind disquieted and distracted with distrustful careful thoughts; polluted with unchaste and wanton thoughts; intoxicated with proud aspiring thoughts; soured and leavened with malicious revengeful thoughts; or at the best diverted from devout and pious thoughts by a thousand impertinencies: Out of the heart proceed evil

thoughts which lie down with us, and rise up
with us, for out of that corrupt fountain, which
wherever we go, we carry about with us, these
streams naturally flow.   Yea, and in the multitude of dreams, as well as many words, there
are also divers vanities, Eccl. v. 2.

And dare we go abroad till we have renewed
our repentance, which we are every night, as
well as every day, thus making work for?
Are we not concerned to confess to him that
knows our hearts, their wanderings from him,
to complain of them to him as revolting and
rebellious hearts, and bent to backslide; to
make our peace in the blood of Christ, and to
pray, that the thoughts of our heart may be
forgiven us? We cannot with safety go into
the business of the day under the guilt of any
sin unrepented of, or unpardoned.

8. In the morning we are addressing ourselves to the work of the day, and therefore are
concerned by prayer to seek God for his presence and blessing; we come, and are encouraged to come boldly to the throne of grace, not
only for mercy to pardon what has been amiss,
but for grace to help in every time of need:
And what time is it that is not a time of need
with us? And therefore what morning should
pass without morning prayer? We read of
that which the duty of every day requires,
Ezra iii. 4, and in reference to that we must

go to God every morning to pray for the gracious disposals of his providence concerning us, and the gracious operations of his Spirit upon us.

We have families to look after it may be, and to provide for, and are in care to do well for them ; let us then every morning by prayer commit them to God, put them under the conduct and government of his grace, and then we effectually put them under the care and protection of his providence. Holy Job rose up early in the morning to offer burnt-offerings for his children, and we should do so to offer up prayers and supplications for them, according to the number of them all, Job i. 5. Thus we cause the blessing to rest on our houses.

We are going about the business of our callings, perhaps, let us look up to God in the first place, for wisdom and grace to manage them well, in the fear of God, and to abide with him in them ; and then we may in faith beg of him to prosper and succeed us in them, to strengthen us for the services of them, to support us under the fatigues of them, to direct the designs of them, and to give us comfort in the gains of them. We have journeys to go, it may be, let us look up to God for his presence with us, and go not whither, where we cannot in faith beg of God to go with us.

We have a prospect perhaps of opportunities of doing or getting good, let us look up to God for a heart to every price in our hands, for skill, and will, and courage, to improve it, that it may not be as a price in the hand of a fool. Every day has its temptations too, some perhaps we foresee, but there may be many more that we think not of, and are therefore concerned to be earnest with God; that we may not be led into any temptation, but guarded against every one; that whatever company we come into, we may have wisdom to do good, and no hurt to them; and to get good, and no hurt by them.

We know not what a day may bring forth; little think in the morning what tidings we may hear, and what events may befall us before night, and should therefore beg of God, grace to carry us through the duties and difficulties which we do not foresee, as well as those which we do: that in order to our standing complete in all the will of God, as the day is, so the strength shall be. We shall find that sufficient unto the day is the evil thereof, and that therefore, as it is folly to take thought for to-morrow's event, so it is wisdom to take thought for to-day's duty, that sufficient unto this day, and the duty of it, may be the supplies of the divine grace thoroughly to furnish us for every good word and work, and thoroughly to fortify us against every evil word or work; that we may not think of, or speak,

or do anything all day, which we may have
cause upon any account to wish unthought,
unspoke, and undone again at night.

For Application

First, Let this word put us in mind of our
omissions; for omissions are sins, and must
come into judgment; how often has our morning worship been either neglected or negli-
gently performed. The work has been either
not done at all, or done deceitfully; either no
sacrifice at all brought, or it has been the torn,
and the lame, and the sick ; either no prayer,
or the prayer not directed aright, nor lifted up.
We have had the morning's mercies, God has
not been wanting in the compassion and care
of a father for us, yet we have not done the
morning's service, but have been shamefully
wanting in the duty of children to him.

Let us be truly humbled before God this
morning for our sin and folly herein, that we
have so often robbed God of the honor, and
ourselves of the benefit of our morning worship. God hath come into our closets, seeking
this fruit, but has found none, or next to none,
hath hearkened and heard, but either we spake
not to him at all, or spake not aright. Some
trifling thing or other has served for an excuse
to put it by once, and when once the good

usage has been broken in upon, conscience has been wounded, and its bones weakened, and we have grown more and more cool to it, and perhaps by degrees it has been quite left off.

Secondly, I beseech you, suffer a word of exhortation concerning this. I know what an influence it would have upon the prosperity of your souls to be constant and sincere in your secret worship, and therefore give me leave to press it upon you with all earnestness ; let God hear from you every morning, every morning let your prayer be directed to him, and look up.

1. Make conscience of your secret worship; keep it up, not only because it has been a custom you have received by tradition from your fathers, but because it is a duty, concerning which you have received commandments from the Lord. Keep up stated times for it, and be true to them. Let those that have hitherto lived in total neglect, or in the frequent omission of secret prayer, be persuaded from henceforward to look upon it as the most needful part of their daily business, and the most delightful part of their daily comfort, and do it accordingly with a constant care, and yet with a constant pleasure.

No persons that have the use of their reason, can pretend an exemption from this duty;

what is said to some is said to all, Pray, pray, continue in prayer, and watch in the same. Rich people are not so much bound to labor with their hands as the poor, poor people are not so much bound to give alms as the rich, but both are equally bound to pray. The rich are not above the necessity of the duty, nor the poor below acceptance with God in it. It is not too soon for the youngest to begin to pray; and those whom the multitude of years has taught wisdom, yet at their end will be fools, if they think they have now no further occasion for prayer.

Let none plead they cannot pray; if you were ready to perish with hunger, you could beg and pray for food, and if you see yourselves undone by reason of sin, can you not beg and pray for mercy and grace? Art thou a Christian? Never for shame say, Thou canst not pray, for that is as absurd as for a soldier to say, he knows not how to handle a sword, or a carpenter an axe. What are you called for into the fellowship of Christ, but that by him you may have fellowship with God. You cannot pray so well as others, pray as well as you can, and God will accept of you.

Let none plead they have no time in a morning for prayer; I dare say, you can find time for other things that are less needful; you had better take time from sleep, than want time for

prayer; and how can you spend time better,
and more to your satisfaction and advantage?
All the business of the day will prosper the better, for your beginning it thus with God.

Let none plead, that they have not a convenient place to be private in for this work;
Isaac retired into the field to pray; and the
Psalmist could be alone with God in a corner
of the house-top. If you cannot perform it
with so much secrecy as you would, yet perform it; it is doing it with ostentation, that is
the fault, not doing it under observation, when
it cannot be avoided. I remember when I was
a young man, coming up hither to London in
the stage coach, in King James's time, there
happened to be a gentleman in the company,
that then was not afraid to own himself a
jesuit; many rencounters he and I had upon
the road, and this was one; he was praising
the custom in popish countries of keeping the
church doors always open, for people to go into
at any time to say their prayers: I told him it
looked too like the practice of the Pharisees, that
prayed in the synagogues; and did not agree
with Christ's command, thou when thou pray-
est thyself, enter not into the church with the
doors open, but into thy closet and shut thy
doors; when he was pressed with that argu-
ment he replied with some vehemence, I believe
you Protestants say your prayers nowhere;

for (said he) I have travelled a great deal in the
coach in company with Protestants, have often
lain in inns in the same room with them, and
have carefully watched them, and could never
perceive that any of them said his prayers
night and morning but one, and he was a
Presbyterian. I hope there was more malice
than truth in what he said; but I mention it
as an intimation, that though we cannot be so
private as we would be in our devotions, yet we
must not omit them, lest the omission should
prove not a sin only, but a scandal.

2. Make a business of your secret worship,
and be not slothful in this business, but fervent
in spirit, serving the Lord. Take heed lest it
degenerate into a formality, and you grow cus-
tomary in your accustomed services. Go about
the duty solemnly. Be inward with God in
it; it is not enough to say your prayers, but
you must pray your prayers, must pray in
praying, as Elijah did, James v. 17. Let us
learn to labor frequently in prayer, as Epaph-
ras did, Col. iv. 12, and we shall find it is the
hand of the diligent in this duty that maketh
rich. God looks not at the length of your
prayers, nor shall you be heard for your much
speaking or fine speaking; but God requires
truth in the inward part, and it is the prayer
of the upright that is his delight. When you
have prayed look upon yourselves as thereby

engaged and encouraged, both to serve God and to trust in him; that the comfort and benefit of your morning devotions may not be as the morning cloud which passeth away, but as the morning light which shines more and more.

DISCOURSE II

SHOWING

HOW TO SPEND THE DAY WITH GOD

————On thee do I wait all the day.—Psalm xxv. 5

WHICH of us is there that can truly say thus! That lives this life of communion with God, which is so much our business, and so much our blessedness? How far short do we come of the spirit of holy David, though we have much better assistance for our acquaintance with God, than the saints then had by the clearer discoveries of the mediation of Christ. Yet that weak Christians who are sincere may not therefore despair, be it remembered, that David himself was not always in such a frame as that he could say so; he had his infirmities, and yet was a man after God's own heart: We have ours, which if they be sincerely lamented and striven against, and the habitual bent of our souls be towards God and heaven, we shall be accepted through Christ, for we are not under the law, but under grace.

However David's profession in the text, shows us what should be our practice, on God we must wait all the day. That notes two things, a patient expectation, and a constant attendance.

1. It speaks a patient expectation of his coming to us in a way of mercy; and then, all the day must be taken figuratively, for all the time that the wanted and desired mercy is delayed. David in the former part of the verse, prayed for divine conduct and instruction, Lead me in thy truth and teach me; he was at a loss, and very desirous to know what God would have him to do, and was ready to do it; but God kept him in suspense, he was not yet clear what was the mind and will of God, what course he should steer, and how he should dispose of himself; will he therefore proceed without divine direction? No: on thee will I wait all the day, as Abraham attended on his sacrifice from morning till the sun went down, before God gave him an answer to his inquiries concerning his seed, Gen. xv. 5, 12, and as Habakkuk stood upon his watch-tower, to see what answer God would give him, when he consulted his oracle; and though it do not come presently, yet at the end it shall speak, and not lie.

David in the words next before the text, had called God the God of his salvation, the God

on whom he depended for salvation, temporal
and eternal salvation, from whom he expected
deliverance out of his present distresses, those
troubles of his heart that were enlarged, *ver.*
17, and out of the hands of those enemies that
were ready to triumph over him, *ver.* 2, and
that hated him with cruel hatred, *ver.* 19.
Hoping that God will be his Saviour, he re-
solves to wait on him all the day, like a genu-
ine son of Jacob, whose dying profession was,
Gen. xlix. 18, I have waited for thy salvation
O Lord.   Sometimes God prevents his people
with the blessings of his goodness, before they
call he answers them, is in the midst of his
church, to help her, and that right early, Psal.
xlvi. 5.   But at other times he seems to stand
afar off, he delays the deliverance, and keeps
them long in expectation of it, nay, and in
suspense about it : the light is neither clear
nor dark, it is day, and that is all; it is a
cloudy and dark day, and it is not till evening
time, that it is light, that the comfort comes
which they have been kept all the day waiting for ; nay, perhaps it comes not till far in
the night, it is at midnight that the cry is
made, Behold the bridegroom comes; the deliverance of the church out of her troubles, the
success of her struggles, and rest from them, a
rescue from under the rod of the wicked, and
the accomplishment of all that which God hath

promised concerning it, is what we must continue humbly waiting upon God for without distrust or impatience; we must wait all the day.

1. Though it be a long day; though we be kept waiting a great while, quite beyond our own reckoning. Though when we have waited long, we are still put to wait longer, and are bid with the prophet's servant to go yet seven times (1 Kings xviii. 43) before we perceive the least sign of mercy coming. We looked that this and the other had been he that should have delivered Israel, but are disappointed; the harvest is past, the summer is ended, and we are not saved, Jer. viii. 20. The time is prolonged, nay, the opportunities are let slip, the summer time and harvest time, when we thought to have reaped the fruit of all our prayers and pains, and patience, is past and ended, and we are as far as ever from salvation; the time that the ark abode in Kirjath-jearim, was long, much longer than it was thought it would have been, when it was first lodged there; it was twenty years; so that the whole house of Israel lamented after the Lord, and began to fear it would abide forever in that obscurity, 1 Sam. vii. 2.

But though it be a long day, it is but a day, but one day, and it is known to the Lord, Zech. xiv. 7. It seems long while we are kept waiting, but the happy issue will enable us to reflect upon it as short, and but for a moment. It is no longer than God hath appointed, and we are sure his time is the best time; and his favors are worth waiting for. The time is long, but it is nothing to the days of eternity, when those that had long patience shall be recompensed for it with an everlasting salvation.

2. Though it be a dark day, yet let us wait upon God all the day. Though while we are kept waiting for what God will do, we are kept in the dark concerning what he is doing, and what is best for us to do, yet let us be content to wait in the dark. Though we see not our signs, though there is none to tell us how long, yet let us resolve to wait, how long soever it be; for though what God doth, we know not now, yet we shall know hereafter, when the mystery of God shall be finished.

Never was man more at a plunge concerning God's dealings with him than poor Job was; I go forward, but he is not there; backward, but I cannot perceive him, on the left hand, on the right hand, but I cannot see him, Job xxiii. 8, 9, yet he sits down, *ver.* 10, resolving to wait on God all the day with a satisfaction in this, that though I know not the way that he takes, he knows the way that I take, and when he has tried me, I shall come forth as gold, approved, and improved. He sits by as a refiner, and will take care that the gold be in the furnace, no longer than is needful for the refining of it. When God's way is in the sea, so that he cannot be traced, yet we are sure his way is in the sanctuary, so that he may be trusted, see Psal. lxxvii. 13, 19. And when clouds and darkness are round about him, yet even then justice and judgment are the habitation of his throne.

3. Though it be a stormy day, yet we must wait upon God all the day. Though we are not only becalmed, and do not get forward, but though the wind be contrary, and drives us back, nay, though it be boisterous, and the church be tossed with tempests, and ready to sink, yet we must hope the best; yet we must wait and weather the storm by patience. It is some comfort, that Christ is in the ship, the church's cause is Christ's own cause, he has espoused it; and he will own it; he is embarked in the same bottom with his people, and therefore, why are ye fearful; doubt not but the ship will come safe to land; though Christ seem for the present to be asleep, the prayers of his disciples will awake him, and he will rebuke the winds and the waves; though the bush burn, if God be in it, it shall not be consumed. Yet this is not all, Christ is not only in the ship, but at the helm; whatever threat-

ens the church, is ordered by the Lord Jesus, and shall be made to work for its good. It is excellently expressed by Mr. George Herbert:

> Away despair, my gracious God doth hear,
>   When winds and waves assault my keel,
> He doth preserve it, he doth steer,
>   Even when the boat seems most to reel.
> Storms are the triumph of his art,
> Well may he close his eyes, but not his heart.

It is a seasonable word at this day; what God will do with us we cannot tell; but this we are sure, he is a God of judgment, infinitely wise and just, and therefore blessed are all they that wait for him, Isa. xxx. 18. He will do his own work in his own way and time; and though we be hurried back into the wilderness, when we thought we had been upon the borders of Canaan, we suffer justly for our unbelief and murmurings, but God acts wisely, and will be found faithful to his promise; his time to judge for his people, and to repent himself concerning his servants, is, when he sees that their strength is gone. This was seen of old in the mount of the Lord, and shall be again. And therefore let us continue in a waiting frame. Hold out faith and patience, for it is good that a man should both hope and quietly wait for the salvation of the Lord.

2. It speaks a constant attendance upon

him in a way of duty.   And so we understand
the day literally; it was David's practice to
wait upon God all the day, MURLB, it signifies
both every day, and all the day long; it is the
same with that command, Prov. xxiii. 17, Be
thou in the fear of the Lord all the day long.

Doct. It is not enough for us to begin every
day with God, but on him we must wait
every day, and all the day long.

For the opening of this I must show, (1.)
What it is to wait upon God; And, (2.) That
we must do this every day, and all the day
long.

For the first, Let us inquire, what it is to
wait on God.   You have heard how much it
is our duty in the morning to speak to him, in
solemn prayer.   But have we then done with
him for all day ?   No, we must still be waiting
on him ; as one to whom we stand very nearly
related, and very strongly obliged.   To wait
on God is to live a life of desire towards him,
delight in him, dependence on him, and devotedness to him.

1. It is to live a life of desire towards God ;
to wait on him, as the beggar waits on his
benefactor, with earnest desire to receive supplies from him; as the sick and sore in Be-
thesda's pool, waited for the stirring of the

water, and attended in the porches with desire to be helped in and healed. When the
prophet had said, Lord, in the way of thy
judgments we have waited for thee, he ex-
plained himself thus in the next words, the
desire of our soul is to thy name, and to the
remembrance of thee ; and with my soul have
I desired thee, Isa. xxvi. 8, 9. Our desire
must be not only towards the good things
that God gives, but towards God himself, his
favor and love, the manifestation of his name
to us, and the influences of his grace upon us.
Then we wait on God, when our souls pant
after him, and his favor, when we thirst for
God, for the living God ; O that I may behold
the beauty of the Lord ! O that I may taste
his goodness ! O that I may bear his image,
and be entirely conformed to his will ! For
there is none in heaven or earth, that I can
desire in comparison of him. O that I may
know him more, and love him better, and be
brought nearer to him, and made fitter for him.
Thus upon the wings of holy desire should our
souls be still soaring upwards towards God,
still pressing forward, forward towards heaven.

We must not only pray solemnly in the
morning, but that desire which is the life and
soul of prayer, like the fire upon the altar,
must be kept continually burning, ready for
the sacrifices that are to be offered upon it.

The bent and bias of the soul in all its motions must be towards God, the serving of him in all we do, and the enjoying of him in all we have. And this is principally intended in the commands given us to pray always, to pray without ceasing, to continue in prayer. Even when we are not making actual addresses to God, yet we must have habitual inclinations towards him; as a man in health, though he is not always eating, yet has always a disposition in him towards the nourishments and delights of the body. Thus must we be always waiting on God, as our chief good, and moving towards him.

2. It is to live a life of delight in God, as the lover waits on his beloved.. Desire is love in motion, as a bird upon the wing; delight is love at rest, as a bird upon the nest; now though our desire must still be so towards God, as that we must be wishing for more of God, yet our delights must be so in God, as that we must never wish for more than God. Believing him to be a God all-sufficient, in him we must be entirely satisfied; let him be mine, and I have enough. Do we love to love God? Is it a pleasure to us to think that there is a God, that he is such a one as he has revealed himself to be, that he is our God by creation to dispose of us as he pleaseth, our God in covenant to dispose of all for the best to us; this is

waiting on our God, always looking up to him
with pleasure.

Something or other the soul has that it
values itself by, something or other that it re-
poses itself in ; and what is it ? God or the
world ? What is it that we pride ourselves
in ? Which we make the matter of our boast-
ing ? It is the character of worldly people,
that they boast themselves in the multitude of
their riches, Psal. xlix. 6, and of their own
might, and the power of their own hands,
which they think has gotten them this wealth ;
it is the character of godly people, that in God
they boast all the day long, Psal. xliv, 8.
That is waiting on God ; having our eye always upon him with a secret complacency, as
men have upon that which is their glory, and
which they glory in.

What is it that we please ourselves with,
which we embrace with the greatest satisfaction, in the bosom of which we lay our heads,
and in having which we hug ourselves, as
having all we would have : the worldly man
when his barns are full of corn, saith, Soul,
take thine ease, eat, drink, and be merry ; the
godly man can never say so till he finds his
heart full of God, and Christ, and grace ; and
then, return unto thy rest, O my soul, here repose thyself; the gracious soul dwells in God,
is at home in him, and there dwells at ease, is

in him perpetually pleased ; and whatever he meets with in the world to make him uneasy, he finds enough in God to balance it.

3. It is to live a life of dependence on God, as the child waits on his father, whom he has a confidence in, and on whom he casts all his care. To wait on God is to expect all good to come to us from him, as the worker of all good for us, and in us, the giver of all good to us, and the protector of us from all evil. Thus David explains himself, Psal. lxii. 5. My soul wait thou only upon God, and continue still to do so, for my expectation is from him, I look not to any other for the good I need ; for I know that every creature is that to me, and no more than he makes it to be, and from him every man's judgment proceeds. Shall we lift up our eyes to the hills ? Doth our help come from thence ? Doth the dew that waters the valleys come no further, than from the tops of the hills ? Shall we go hither, and lift up our eyes to the heavens, to the clouds ? Can they of themselves give rain ? No, if God hear not the heavens, they hear not the earth ; we must therefore look above the hills, above the heavens, for all our help cometh from the Lord ; it was the acknowledgment of a king, and no good one neither, if the Lord do not help thee, whence shall I help thee out of the barn-floor, or out of the wine press ?

And our expectations from God as far as they are guided by, and grounded upon the word which he hath spoken, ought to be humbly confident and with a full assurance of faith. We must know and be sure, that no word of God shall fall to the ground, that the expectation of the poor shall not perish. Worldly people say to their gold, thou art my hope; and to the fine gold, thou art my confidence, and the rich man's wealth is his strong city; but God is the only refuge and portion of the godly man here in the land of the living; it is to him only that he saith, and he saith it with a holy boldness, Thou art my hope, and my confidence. The eyes of all things wait on him, for he is good to all; but the eyes of his saints especially, for he is in a peculiar manner good to Israel, good to them. They know his name and therefore will trust, and triumph in him, as those that know they shall not be made ashamed of their hope.

4. It is to live a life of devotedness to God, as the servant waits on his master, ready to observe his will, and to do his work, and in everything to consult his honor and interest. To wait on God, is entirely and unreservedly to refer ourselves to his wise and holy directions, and disposals, and cheerfully to acquiesce in them, and comply with them. The servant that waits on his master, chooseth not his own

way, but follows his master step by step: thus must we wait on God, as those that have no will of our own, but what is wholly resolved into his; and must therefore study to accommodate ourselves to his. It is the character of the redeemed of the Lord, that they follow the Lamb wheresoever he goes, with an implicit faith and obedience. As the eyes of a servant are to the hand of his master, and the eyes of a maiden to the hand of her mistress, so must our eyes wait on the Lord, to do what he appoints us, to take what he allots us; Father, thy will be done; Master, thy will be done.

The servant waits on his master, not only to do him service, but to do him honor; and thus must we wait on God that we may be to him for a name, and for a praise. His glory must be our ultimate end, to which we, and all we are, have, and can do, must be dedicated; we must wear his livery, attend in his courts, and follow his motions as his servants, for this end, that he may in all things be glorified.

To wait on God, is to make his will our rule.

1. To make the will of his precept, the rule of our practice, and to do every duty with an eye to that. We must wait on him to receive his commands, with a resolution to comply with them, how much soever they may contradict our corrupt inclinations, or secular

interests. We must wait on him, as the holy
angels do, that always behold the face of their
Father, as those that are at his beck, and are
ready to go upon the least intimation of his will,
though but by a wink of his eye, wherever he
sends them. Thus must we do the will of
God, as the angels do it that are in heaven,
those ministers of his that do his pleasure, and
are always about his throne in order to it;
never out of the way.

David here prays, that God would show him
his way, and lead him, and teach him, and
keep him, and forward him in the way of his
duty; and so the text comes in as a plea to
enforce that petition, for on thee do I wait all
the day; ready to receive the law from thy
mouth, and in everything to observe thine orders. And then it intimates this, that those
and those only can expect to be taught of God,
who are ready and willing to do as they are
taught. If any man will do his will, be stead-
fastly resolved in the strength of his grace to
comply with it, he shall know what his will is.
David prays, Lord, give me understanding,
and then promiseth himself, I shall keep thy
law, yea I shall observe it; as the servant that
waits on his master. They that go up to the
house of the Lord, with an expectation that he
will teach them his ways, it must be with a
humble resolution, that they will walk in his

paths, Isa. ii. 3. Lord, let the pillar of cloud and fire go before me, for I am determined with full purpose of heart to follow it, and thus to wait on my God all the day.

2. To make the will of his providence, the rule of our patience, and to bear every affliction with an eye to that. We are sure, it is God that performeth all things for us, and he performeth the thing that is appointed for us; we are sure, that all is well that God doth, and shall be made to work for good to all that love him: and in order to that, we ought to acquiesce in, and accommodate ourselves to the whole will of God. To wait on the Lord, is to say, It is the Lord, let him do with me as seemeth good to him, because nothing seemeth good to him, but what is really good; and so we shall see, when God's work appears in a full light; it is to say, Not as I will, but as thou wilt, for should it be according to my mind? It is to bring our mind to our condition in everything, so as to keep that calm and easy, whatever happens to make us uneasy.

And we must therefore bear the affliction, whatever it is, because it is the will of God; it is what he has allotted to us, who doth all according to the counsel of his own will. This is Christian patience; I was dumb, I opened not my mouth, not because it was to no purpose to complain, but because thou didst it, and therefore I had no reason to complain. And this will reconcile us to every affliction, one as well as another, because whatever it is, it is the will of God; and in compliance with that we must not only be silent, because of the sovereignty of his will, Woe unto him that strives with his Maker; but we must be satisfied, because of the wisdom and goodness of it. Whatever the disposals of God's providence may be concerning those that wait on him, we may be sure that as he doth them no wrong, so he means them no hurt: Nay, they may say as the Psalmist did, even then when he was plagued all the day long, and chastened every morning, however it be, yet God is good; and therefore, Though he slay me, yet will I trust in him, yet will I wait on him.

I might open this duty of waiting on God; by other scripture expressions which speak the same thing, and are, as this, comprehensive of a great part of that homage, which we are bound to pay to him, and that communion which it is our interest to keep up with him. Truly thus our fellowship is with the Father, and with the Son Jesus Christ.

It is to set God always before us, Psal. xvi. 8. To look upon him as one always near us, always at our right hand, and that has his eye upon us, wherever we are and whatever we are doing; nay, as one in whom we live, and move, and have our being, with whom we have to do, and to whom we are accountable. This is pressed upon us, as the great principle of Gospel obedience; walk before me, and be thou upright; herein consists that uprightness which is our evangelical perfection, in walking at all times as before God, and studying to approve ourselves to him.

It is to have our eyes ever towards the Lord, as it follows here, Psal. xxv. 15. Though we cannot see him by reason of our present distance and darkness, yet we must look towards him, towards the place where his honor dwells; as those that desire the knowledge of him and his will, and direct all to his honor as the mark we aim at, laboring in this, that whether present or absent we may be accepted of him. To wait on him, is to follow him with our eye in all those things wherein he is pleased to manifest himself, and to admit the discoveries of his being and perfections.

It is to acknowledge God in all our ways, Prov. iii. 6, in all the actions of life, and in all the affairs of life, we must walk in his hand, and set ourselves in the way of his steps. In all our undertakings, we must wait upon him for direction and success, and by faith and prayer commit our way to him to undertake for us; and him we must take with us where ever we go; If thy presence go not up with us, carry us not up hence. In all our comforts we must see his hand giving them out to us, and in all our crosses we must see the same hand laying them upon us, that we may learn to receive both good and evil, and to bless the name of the Lord both when he gives and when he takes.

It is to follow the Lord fully, as Caleb did, Numb. xiv. 24. It is to fulfil after the Lord, so the word is; to have respect to all his commandments, and to study to stand complete in his whole will. Wherever God leads us and goes before us, we must be followers of him as dear children, must follow the Lamb whithersoever he goes, and take him for our guide whithersoever we go.

This is to wait on God, and those that do so may cheerfully wait for him, for he will without fail appear in due time to their joy, and that word of Solomon shall be made good to them; he that waits on his master shall be honored, for Christ has said, where I am, there shall also my servant be, Prov. xxvii. 18.

For the second thing. Having showed you what it is to wait on God, I come next to show, that this we must do every day; and all the day long.

1. We must wait on our God every day. *Omni die,* so some. This is the work of every

day, which is to done in its day, for the duty
of every day requires it. Servants in the courts
of princes have their weeks, or months of waiting appointed them, and are tied to attend only
at certain times. But God's servants must
never be out of waiting: all the days of our
appointed time, the time of our work and war-
fare here on earth. we must be waiting, Job
xiv. 14, and not desire or expect to be discharged from this attendance, till we come to
heaven, where we shall wait on God, as angels
do, more nearly and constantly.

We must wait on God every day.

1. Both on Sabbath days, and on week days.
The Lord's day is instituted and appointed
on purpose for our attendance on God in the
courts of his house, there we must wait on
him, to give glory to him, and to receive both
commands, and favors from him; ministers
must then wait on their ministry, Rom. xii. 7,
and people must wait on it too, saying as Cornelius for himself and his friends, now we are
all here ready before God, to hear all things
that are commanded thee of God, Acts x. 33.
It is for the honor of God to help to fill up the
assemblies of those that attend at the footstool
of his throne, and to add to their number.
The whole Sabbath time except what is taken
up in works of necessity and mercy, must be
employed in waiting on our God. Christians

are spiritual priests, and as such it is their business to wait in God's house at the time appointed.

But that is not enough ; we must wait upon
our God on week days too, for every day of
the week we want mercy from him, and have
work to do for him. Our waiting upon him
in public ordinances on the first day of the
week, is designed to fix us to, and fit us for
communion with him all the week after ; so
that we answer not the intentions of the Sabbath, unless the impressions of it abide upon
us, and go with us into the business of the
week, and be kept always in the imagination
of the thoughts of our heart. Thus from one
Sabbath to another, and from one new moon
to another, we must keep in a holy gracious
frame ; must be so in the Spirit on the Lord's
day, as to walk in the Spirit all the week.

2. Both on idle days, and busy days, we
must be found waiting on God. Some days
of our lives are days of labor and hurry, when
our particular calling calls for our close and
diligent application ; but we must not think
that will excuse us from our constant attendance on God. Even then when our hands are
working about the world, our hearts may be
waiting on our God, by an habitual regard to
him, to his providence as our guide, and his
glory as our end, in our worldly business : and

thus we must abide with him in them. Those
that rise up early, and sit up late, and eat the
bread of carefulness in pursuit of the world,
yet are concerned to wait on God, because
otherwise all their care and pains will signify
nothing ; it is labor in vain, Psal. cxxvii. 1, 2,
nay, it is labor in the fire.

Some days of our lives we relax from business, and take our ease. Many of you have
your time for diversion, but then when you
lay aside other business, this of waiting upon
God must not be laid aside. When you prove
yourselves with mirth, as Solomon did, and
say, you will enjoy pleasure a little, yet let
this wisdom remain with you, Eccl. ii. 1, 3, let
your eye be then up to God, and take heed of
dropping your communion with him, in that
which you call an agreeable conversation with
your friends. Whether it be a day of work, or
a day of rest, we shall find nothing like waiting upon God both to enlighten the toil of our
work, and to sweeten the comfort of our repose.
So that whether we have much to do, or little
to do in the world, still we must wait upon
God, that we may be kept from the temptation that attends both the one and the other.

3. Both in days of prosperity, and in days
of adversity, we must be found waiting upon
God. Doth the world smile upon us, and court
us ? Yet let us not turn from attending on

God, to make our court to it: If we have
never so much of the wealth of the world, yet
we cannot say we have no need of God, no
further occasion to make use of him, as David
was ready to say, when in his prosperity he
said he should never be moved ; but soon saw
his error, when God hid his face, and he was
troubled, Psal. xxx. 6. When our affairs prosper, and into our hands God bringeth plenti-
fully, we must wait upon God as our great
landlord, and own our obligations to him;
must beg his blessing on what we have, and
his favor with it, and depend upon him both
for the continuance, and for the comfort of it.
We must wait upon God for wisdom and grace,
to use what we have in the world for the ends
for which we are intrusted with it, as those
that must give account, and know not how
soon. And how much soever we have of this
world, and how richly soever it is given us to
enjoy it, still we must wait upon God for better
things, not only than the world gives, but than
he himself gives in this world. Lord put me
not off with this for a portion.

And when the world frowns upon us, and
things go very cross, we must not so fret ourselves at its frowns, or so frighten ourselves
with them, as thereby to be driven off from
waiting on God, but rather let us thereby be
driven to it. Afflictions are sent for this end,

to bring us to the throne of grace, to teach us to pray, and to make the word of God's grace precious to us. In the day of our sorrow we must wait upon God for those comforts which are sufficient to balance our grief; Job, when in tears, fell down and worshipped God, taking away, as well as giving. In the day of our fear we must wait upon God for those encouragements that are sufficient to silence our fears; Jehoshaphat, in his distress waited on God, and was not in vain, his heart was established by it; and so was David's often, which brought him to this resolution, which was an anchor to his soul, What time I am afraid, I will trust in thee.

4. Both in the days of youth, and in the days of old age, we must be found waiting on God. Those that are young cannot begin their attendance on God too soon: The child Samuel ministered to the Lord, and the scripture story puts a particular mark of honor upon it; and Christ was wonderfully pleased with the hosannas of the children that waited on him, when he rode in triumph into Jerusalem: When Solomon in his youth, upon his accession to the throne, waited upon God for wisdom, it is said, the saying pleased the Lord. I remember thee (saith God to Israel) even the kindness of thy youth, when thou wentest after me, and didst wait upon me in a wilder-

ness, Jer. ii. 2. To wait upon God, is to be mindful of our Creator, and the proper time for that is in the days of our youth, Eccl. xii. 1. Those that would wait upon God aright, must learn betimes to do it; the most accomplished courtiers are those that are bred at court.

And may the old servants of Jesus be dismissed from waiting on him? No, their attendance is still required, and shall be still accepted: they shall not be cast off by their Master in the time of old age, and therefore let not them then desert his service. When through the infirmities of age they can no longer be working servants in God's family, yet they may be waiting servants. Those that like Barzillai are unfit for the entertainments of the courts of earthly princes, yet may relish the pleasures of God's courts as well as ever. The Levites when they were past the age of fifty, and were discharged from the toilsome part of their ministration, yet still must wait on God, must be quietly waiting, to give honor to him, and to receive comfort from him. Those that have done the will of God, and their doing work is at an end, have need of patience to enable them to wait till they inherit the promise: and the nearer the happiness is which they are waiting for, the dearer should the God be they are waiting on, and hope shortly to be with, to be with eternally.

2. We must wait on our God all the day, to die, so we read it. Every day from morning to night we must continue waiting on God; whatever change there may be of our employment, this must be the constant disposition of our souls, we must attend upon God, and have our eyes ever towards him; we must not at any time allow ourselves to wander from God, or to attend on anything besides him, but what we attend on for him; in subordination to his will, and in subserviency to his glory.

1. We must cast our daily cares upon him. Every day brings with it its fresh cares, more or less, these wake with us every morning, and we need not go so far forward as to-morrow to fetch care, sufficient unto the day is the evil thereof: you that are great dealers in the world, have your cares attending you all the day; though you keep them to yourselves, yet they sit down with you, and rise up with you; they go out and come in with you, and are more a load upon you than those you converse with are aware of. Some, through the weakness of their spirits, can scarce determine anything but with fear and trembling.

Let this burden be cast upon the Lord, believing that his providence extends itself to all your affairs, to all events concerning you, and to all the circumstances of them, even the most minute, and seemingly accidental; that

your times are in his hand, and all your ways
at his disposal; believe his promise, that all
things shall be made to work for good to those
that love him, and then refer it to him in
everything, to do with you and yours as seemeth good in his eyes, and rest satisfied in having done so, and resolve to be easy. Bring
your cares to God by prayer in the morning,
spread them before him, and then make it to
appear all the day, by the composedness and
cheerfulness of your spirits, that you left them
with him as Hannah did, who, when she had
prayed, went her way and did eat, and her
countenance was no more sad, 1 Sam. i. 18.
Commit your way to the Lord, and then submit to his disposal of it, though it may cross
your expectations; and bear up yourselves
upon the assurance God has given you, that
he will care for you as the tender father for
the child.

2. We must manage our daily business for
him, with an eye to his providence, putting us
into the calling and employment wherein we
are; and to his precept, making diligence in it
our duty; with an eye to his blessing, as that
which is necessary to make it comfortable and
successful; and to his glory, as our highest
end in all. This sanctifies our common actions to God, and sweetens them, and makes
them pleasant to ourselves. If Gaius brings

his friends that he is parting with, a little way on their journey, it is but a piece of common civility, but let him do it after a godly sort; let him in it pay respect to them, because they belong to Christ, and for his sake ; let him do it that he may have an opportunity of so much more profitable communication with them, and then it becomes an act of Christian piety. 3 John 6. It is a general rule by which we must govern ourselves in the business of every day, Whatever we do in word or deed, to do all in the name of the Lord Jesus, Col. iii. 17, and thus in and by the Mediator we wait on our God.

This is particularly recommended to servants, though their employments are but mean, and they are under the command of their masters according to the flesh, yet let them do their servile works as the servants of Christ, as unto the Lord, and not unto men ; let them do it with singleness of heart as unto Christ, and they shall be accepted of him, and from him shall receive the reward of the inheritance, Eph. vi. 5, 6, 7, 8 ; Col. iii. 22, 24. Let them wait on God all the day, when they are doing their day's work, by doing it faithfully and conscientiously, that they may adorn the doctrine of God our Saviour, by aiming at his glory even in common business: They work that they may get bread, they would get bread that they may live, they would live not that they may live to themselves, and please themselves, but that they may live to God, and please him. They work that they may fill up time, and fill up a place in the world, and because that God who made and maintains us, has appointed us with quietness to work and mind our own business.

3. We must receive our daily comforts from him ; we must wait on him as our benefactor, as the eyes of all things wait upon him, to give them their food in due season, and what he giveth them, that they gather. To him we must look as to our Father for our daily bread, and from him we are appointed to ask it, yea though we have it in the house, though we have it upon the table. We must wait upon him for a covenant right to it, for leave to make use of it, for a blessing upon it, for nourishment by it, and for comfort in it. It is in the word and prayer that we wait on God, and keep up communion with him, and by these every creature of God is sanctified to us, 1 Tim. iv. 4, 5, and the property of it is altered ; to the pure all things are pure ; they have them from the covenant, and not from common providence, which makes a little that the righteous man has, better than the riches of many wicked, and much more valuable and comfortable.

No inducement can be more powerful to
make us see to it, that what we have we get
it honestly, and use it soberly, and give God
his due out of it, than this consideration, that
we have our all from the hand of God, and are
intrusted with it as stewards, and consequently
are accountable. If we have this thought as
a golden thread running through all the comforts of every day, these are God's gifts, every
bit we eat, and every drop we drink is his
mercy, every breath we draw, and every step
we take, is his mercy, this will keep us continually waiting upon him, as the ass on his master's crib, and will put a double sweetness into
all our enjoyments. God will have his mercies taken fresh from his compassions, which
for this reason are said to be new every morning; and therefore it is not once a week that
we are to wait upon him, as people go to mar-
ket to buy provisions for the whole week, but
we must wait on him every day, and all the
day, as those that live from hand to mouth,
and yet live very easy.

4. We must resist our daily temptations,
and do our daily duties in the strength of his
grace. Every day brings its temptations with
it; our Master knew that when he taught us,
as duly as we pray for our daily bread, to pray
that we might not be led into temptation.
There is no business we engage in, no enjoy-

ment we partake of, but it has its snares attending it; Satan by it assaults us, and endeavors to draw us into sin: Now sin is the great evil we should be continually upon our guard against, as Nehemiah was, *ch*. vi. 13. That I should be afraid, and do so, and sin. And we have no way to secure ourselves but by waiting on God all the day, we must not only in the morning put ourselves under the protection of his grace, but we must all day keep ourselves under the shelter of it; must not only go forth, but go on in dependence upon that grace which he hath said shall be sufficient for us, that care which will not suffer us to be tempted above what we are able. Our waiting upon God will furnish us with the best arguments to make use of in resisting temptations, and with strength according to the day; be strong in the Lord, and in the power of his might, and then we wait on the Lord all the day.

We have duty to do, many an opportunity of speaking good words, and doing good works, and we must see and own that we are not sufficient of ourselves for anything that is good, not so much as to think a good thought: we must therefore wait upon God, must seek to him, and depend upon him, for that light and fire, that wisdom and zeal, which is necessary to the due discharge of our duty; that by his

grace we may not only be fortified against
every evil word and work, but furnished for
every good word and work. From the fulness
that is in Jesus Christ, we must by faith be
continually drawing grace for grace, grace for
all gracious exercises; grace to help in every
time of need: We must wait on this grace,
must follow the conduct of it, comply with the
operations of it, and must be turned to it as
wax to the seal.

5. We must bear our daily afflictions with
submission to his will; We are bid to expect
trouble in the flesh, something or other happens every day that grieves us, something in
our relations, something in our callings, events
concerning ourselves, our families, or friends,
that are matter of sorrow : perhaps we have
every day some bodily pain or sickness : or,
some cross and disappointment in our affairs;
now in these we must wait upon God.   Christ
requires it of all his disciples, that they take
up their cross daily, Matth. xvi. 24. We must
not wilfully pluck the cross down upon us, but
must take it up when God lays it in our way,
and not go a step out of the way of duty either
to it, or to miss it. It is not enough to bear
the cross, but we must take it up, we must accommodate ourselves to it, and acquiesce in the
will of God in it. Not, this is an evil, and I
must bear it, because I cannot help it, but this

is an evil, and I will bear it, because it is the will of God.

We must see every affliction allotted us by our heavenly Father, and in it must eye his correcting hand, and therefore must wait on him to know the cause wherefore he contends with us, what the fault is for which we are in this affliction chastened: what the distemper is which is to be by this affliction cured, that we may answer God's end in afflicting us, and so may be made partakers of his holiness. We must attend the motions of providence, keep our eye upon our Father when he frowns, that we may discover what his mind is, and what the obedience is we are to learn, by the things that we suffer. We must wait on God for support under our burthens; must put ourselves into, and stay ourselves upon the everlasting arms, which are laid under the children of God to sustain them, when the rod of God is upon them. And him we must attend for deliverance : must not seek to extricate ourselves by any sinful indirect methods, nor look to creatures for relief, but still wait on the Lord, until that he have mercy on us; well content to bear the burthen until God ease us of it, and ease us in mercy, Psal. cxxiii. 2. If the affliction be lengthened out, yet we must wait upon the Lord, even when he hides his face,

Isa. viii. 17, hoping it is but in a little wrath, and for a small moment, Isa. liv. 7, 8.

6. We must expect the tidings and events of every day, with a cheerful and entire resignation to the divine providence. While we are in this world, we are still expecting, hoping well, fearing ill: we know not what a day or a night, or an hour will bring forth, Prov. xxvii. 1, but it is big with something, and we are too apt to spend our thoughts in vain about things future, which happen quite differently from what we imagined. Now in all our prospects we must wait upon God.

Are we in hopes of good tidings, a good issue? Let us wait on God as the giver of the good we hope for, and be ready to take it from his hand ; and to meet him with suitable affections then when he is coming towards us in a way of mercy. Whatever good we hope for, it is God alone, and his wisdom, power, and goodness, that we must hope in. And therefore our hopes must be humble and modest, and regulated by his will ; what God has promised us, we may with assurance promise ourselves, and no more. If thus we wait on God in our hopes, should the hope be deferred, it would not make the heart sick, no, not if it should be disappointed, for the God we wait on, will overrule all for the best ; but when the desire comes, in prosecution of which we have thus waited on God, we may see it coming from his love, and it will be a tree of life, Prov. xiii. 12.

Are we in fear of evil tidings, of melancholy events, and a sad issue of the depending affair? Let us wait on God to be delivered from all our fears, from the things themselves we are afraid of, and from the amazing tormenting fears of them, Psal. xxxiv. 4. When Jacob was with good reason afraid of his brother Esau, he waited on God, brought his fears to him, wrestled with him, and prevailed for deliverance! What time I am afraid, said David, I will trust in thee, and wait on thee; and that shall establish the heart, shall fix it, so as to set it above the fear of evil tidings.

Are we in suspense between hope and fear, sometimes one prevails, and sometimes the other, let us wait on God, as the God to whom belong the issues of life and death, good and evil; from whom our judgment, and every man's doth proceed, and compose ourselves into a quiet expectation of the event, whatever it may be, with a resolution to accommodate ourselves to it: Hope the best, and get ready for the worst, and then take what God sends.

For Application

First, Let me further urge upon you this

duty of waiting upon God all the day, in some more particular instances, according to what you have to do all the day, in the ordinary business of it. We are weak and forgetful, and need to be put in mind of our duty in general, upon every occasion for the doing of it; and therefore I choose to be thus particular, that I may be your remembrancer.

1. When you meet with your families in the morning, wait upon God for a blessing upon them, and attend him with your thanksgivings for the mercies you and yours have jointly received from God the night past: you and your houses must serve the Lord, must wait on him. See it owing to his goodness who is the founder and father of the families of the righteous, that you are together, that the voice of rejoicing and salvation is in your tabernacles, and therefore wait upon him to continue you together, to make you comforts to one another, to enable you to do the duty of every relation, and to lengthen out the days of your tranquillity. In all the conversation we have with our families, the provision we make for them, and the orders we give concerning them, we must wait upon God, as the God of all the families of Israel, Jer. xxxi. 1. And have an eye to Christ, as he in whom all the families of the earth are blessed.

Every member of the family sharing in

family mercies, must wait on God for grace to contribute to family duties, whatever disagreeableness there may be in any family relation, instead of having the spirit either burthened with it, or provoked by it, let it be an inducement to wait on God, who is able either to redress the grievance, or to balance it, and give grace to bear it.

2. When you are pursuing the education of your children or the young ones under your charge, wait upon God for his grace to make the means of their education successful. When you are yourselves giving them instruction in things pertaining either to life or godliness, their general or particular calling, when you are sending them to school in a morning, or ordering them the business of the day, wait upon God to give them an understanding, and a good capacity for their business. Especially their main business, for it is God that giveth wisdom. If they are but slow, and do not come on as you could wish, yet wait on God to bring them forward, and to give them his grace in his own time, and while you are patiently waiting on him that will encourage you to take pains with them, and will likewise make you patient and gentle towards them.

And let children and young people wait on God in all their daily endeavors, to fit themselves for the service of God in their generation ;

you desire to be comforts to your relations, to be good for something in this world; do you beg of God then a wise and an understanding heart, as Solomon did, and wait upon him all the day for it, that you may be still increasing in wisdom, as you do in stature, and in favor with God and man.

3. When you go to your shops, or apply yourselves to the business of your particular calling, wait upon God for his presence with you. Your business calls for your constant attendance, every day, and all the day; keep thy shop, and thy shop will keep thee; but let your attendance on God in your callings, be as constant as your attendance on your callings. Eye God's providence in all the occurrences of them. Open shop with this thought, I am now in the way of my duty, and I depend upon God to bless me in it. When you are waiting for customers, wait on God to find you something to do in that calling to which he hath called you; those you call chance customers, you should rather call Providence customers, and should say of the advantage you make by them, the Lord my God brought it to me.

When you are buying and selling, see God's eye upon you to observe, whether you are honest and just in your dealings, and do no wrong to those you deal with; and let your

eye then be up to him, for that discretion to
which God doth instruct not only the husband-
man, but the tradesman, Isa. xxviii. 26, that
prudence which directs the way, and with
which it is promised, the good man shall order
his affairs ; for that blessing which makes rich,
and adds no sorrow with it; for that honest
profit which may be expected in the way of
honest diligence.

Whatever your employments be, in country
business, city-business, or sea-business, or only
in the business of the house, go about them in
the fear of God, depending upon him to make
them comfortable, and successful, and to prosper the work of your hands unto you.   And
hereby you will arm yourselves against the
many temptations you are compassed about
with in your worldly business ; by waiting on
God, you will be freed from that care and cum-
ber which attends much serving; will have
your minds raised above the little things of
sense and time, will be serving God then when
you are most busy about the world, and will
have God in your hearts, when your hands are
full of the world.

4. When you take a book in your hands,
God's book, or any other useful good book,
wait upon God for his grace to enable you to
make a good use of it.   Some of you spend a
deal of time every day in reading, and I hope

none of you let a day pass without reading some portions of scripture, either alone or with your families; take heed that the time you spend in sending be not lost time; it is so, if you read that which is idle and vain, and un-profitable; it is so, if you read that which is good, even the word of God itself, and do not mind it, or observe it, or aim to make it of any advantage to you. Wait upon God, who gives you those helps for your souls, to make them helpful indeed to you. The Eunuch did so, when he was reading the book of the prophet Isaiah in his chariot, and God presently sent him one, who made him understand what he read.

You read perhaps now and then the histo-ries of former times; in acquainting yourselves with them, you must have an eye to God, and to that wise and gracious Providence which governed the world before we were born, and preserved the church in it, and therefore may be still depended upon to do all for the best, for he is Israel's king of old.

5. When you sit down to your tables, wait on God, see his hand spreading and preparing a table before you in despite of your enemies, and in the society of your friends; often review the grant which God made to our first father Adam, and in him to us, of the products of the earth, Gen. i. 29. Behold I have given you

every herb bearing seed, bread corn especially,
to you it shall be for meat.   And the grant he
afterwards made to Noah our second father,
and in him to us, Gen. ix. 3.   Every moving
thing that liveth shall be meat for you, even as
the green herb ; and see in those what a boun-
tiful benefactor he is to mankind, and wait
upon him accordingly.

We must eat and drink to the glory of God,
and then we wait on him in eating and drink-
ing.   We must receive nourishment for our
bodies, that we may be fitted to serve our souls
in the service of God, to his honor in this
world.   We must taste covenant-love in common mercies, and enjoy the Creator while we
are using the creature ; we must depend upon
the word of blessing from the mouth of God,
to make our food nourishing to us ; and if our
provisions be mean and scanty, we must make
up the want of them by faith in the promise
of God, and rejoice in him, as the God of our
salvation, though the fig-tree doth not blossom,
and there is no fruit in the vine.

6. When you visit your friends, or receive
their visits, wait upon God ; let your eye be to
him with thankfulness for your friends and
acquaintance, that you have comfort in ; that
the wilderness is not made your habitation, and
the solitary and desert land your dwelling;
that you have comfort not only in your own

houses, but in those of your neighbors, with
whom you have freedom of converse; and that
you are not driven out from among men, and
made a burthen and terror to all about you.
That you have clothing not only for necessity
but for ornament, to go abroad in, is a mercy
which, that we may not pride ourselves in, we
must take notice of God in, I decked thee with
ornaments, saith God, and put ear-rings in
thine ears, Ezek. xvi. 11, 12. That you have
houses, furniture, and entertainment, not only
for yourselves, but for your friends, is a mercy
in which God must be acknowledged.

And when we are in company, we must
look up to God for wisdom to carry ourselves,
so as that we may do much good to, and get
no harm by those with whom we converse;
wait on God for that grace with which our
speech should be always seasoned, by which
all corrupt communication may be prevented,
and we may abound in that which is good,
and to the use of edifying, and which may
minister grace to the hearers, that our lips may
feed many.

7. When you give alms, or do any act of
charity, wait on God, do it as unto him, give
to a disciple in the name of a disciple, to the
poor because they belong to Christ; do it not
for the praise of men, but for the glory of God,
with a single eye, and an upright heart, direct

it to him, and then your alms as well as your prayers, like those of Cornelius, come up for a memorial before God, Acts x. 4. Beg of God to accept what you do for the good of others, that your alms may indeed be offerings, Acts xxiv. 17. May be an odor of a sweet smell, a sacrifice acceptable, well pleasing to God, Phil. iv. 18.

Desire of God a blessing upon what we give in charity, that it may be comfortable to those to whom it is given, and that though what you are able to give is but a little, like the widow's two mites, yet that by God's blessing it may be doubled, and made to go a great way, like the widow's meal in the barrel, and oil in the cruse.

Depend upon God to make up to you what you lay out in good works, and to recompense it abundantly in the resurrection of the just; nay, and you are encouraged to wait upon him, for a return of it even in this life; it is bread cast upon the waters, which you shall find again after many days; and you shall carefully observe the providence of God whether it do not make you rich amends for your good works, according to the promise, that you may understand the loving kindness of the Lord, and his faithfulness to the word which he hath spoken.

8. When you inquire after public news, in

that wait upon God : do it with an eye to him ; for this reason, because you are truly concerned for the interests of his kingdom in the world, and lay them near your hearts ; because you have a compassion for mankind, for the lives and souls of men, and especially of God's people ; ask, what news ? Not as the Athenians, only to satisfy a vain curiosity, and to pass away an idle hour or two, but that you may know how to direct your prayers and praises, and how to balance your hopes and fears, and may gain such an understanding of the times, as to learn what you and others ought to do.

If the face of public affairs be bright and pleasing, wait upon God to carry on and perfect his own work ; and depend not upon the wisdom or strength of any instruments; if it be dark and discouraging, wait upon God to prevent the fears of his people, and to appear for them, when he sees that their strength is gone. In the midst of the greatest successes of the church, and the smiles of second causes, we must not think it needless to wait on God ; and in the midst of its greatest discouragements, when its affairs are reduced to the last extremity, we must not think it fruitless to wait upon God ; for creatures cannot help without him, but he can help without them.

9. When you are going journeys, wait on

God ; put yourselves under his protection, commit yourselves to his care, and depend upon
him to give his angels a charge concerning
you, to bear you up in their arms when you
move, and to pitch their tents about you where
you rest. See how much you are indebted to
the goodness of his providence, for all the comforts and conveniences you are surrounded with
in your travels. It is he that has cast our lot
in a land where we wander not in wildernesses,
as in the deserts of Arabia, but have safe and
beaten roads ; and that through the terrors
of war, the highways are not unoccupied ; to
him we owe it, that the inferior creatures are
serviceable to us, and that our going out and
coming in are preserved ; that when we are
abroad we are not in banishment, but have
liberty to come home again ; and when we are
at home we are not under confinement, but
have liberty to go abroad.

We must therefore have our eyes up to God
at our setting out, Lord, go along with me
where I go ; under his shelter we must travel,
confiding in his care of us, and encouraging
ourselves with that in all the dangers we meet
with ; and in our return must own his goodness ; all our bones must say, Lord who is like
unto thee, for he keepeth all our bones, not one
of them is broken.

10. When we retire into solitude, to be

alone, walking in the fields, or alone reposing ourselves in our closets, still we must be waiting on God; still we must keep up our communion with him, when we are communing with our own hearts. When we are alone, we must not be alone, but the Father must be with us, and we with him. We shall find temptations even in solitude, which we have need to guard against; Satan set upon our Saviour, when he was alone in a wilderness; but there also we have an opportunity, if we but know how to improve it, for that devout, that divine contemplation, which is the best conversation, so that we may never be less alone than when alone. If when we sit alone and keep silence, withdrawn from business and conversation, we have but the art, I should say the heart, to fill up those vacant minutes with pious meditations of God and divine things, we then gather up the fragments of time which remain, that nothing may be lost, and so are we found waiting on God all the day.

Secondly, Let me use some motives to persuade you, thus to live a life of communion with God, by waiting on him all the day.

1. Consider, the eye of God is always upon you. When we are with our superiors, and observe them to look upon us, that engageth us to look upon them; and shall we not then

look up to God, whose eyes always behold, and whose eyelids try the children of men ? He sees all the motions of our hearts, and sees with pleasure the motions of our hearts towards him, which should engage us to set him always before us.

The servant, though he be careless at other times, yet when he is under his master's eye, will wait in his place, and keep close to his business ; we need no more to engage us to diligence, than to do our work with eye-service while our master looks on, and because he doth so, for then we shall never look off.

2. The God you are to wait on, is one with whom you have to do, Heb. iv. 13. All things, even the thoughts and intents of the heart, are naked and open unto the eyes of him with whom we have to do; PROS ON EMINO LOGOS, *with whom we have business, or word,* who hath something to say to us, and to whom we have something to say ; or as some read it, to whom for us there is an account ; there is a reckoning, a running account between us and him : And we must every one of us shortly give account of ourselves to him, and of everything done in the body, and therefore are concerned to wait on him ; that all may be made even daily between us and him in the blood of Christ, which balanceth the account. Did we consider how much we have to do with

God every day, we would be more diligent and constant in our attendance on him.

3. The God we are to wait upon, continually waits to be gracious to us; he is always doing us good, prevents us with the blessings of his goodness, daily loads us with his benefits, and slips no opportunity of showing his care of us when we are in danger; his bounty to us when we are in want; and his tenderness for us when we are in sorrow. His good providence waits on us all the day, to preserve our going out and our coming in, Isa. xxx. 18, to give us relief and succor in due season, to be seen in the mount of the Lord. Nay, his good grace waits on us all the day, to help us in every time of need; to be strength to us according as the day is, and all the occurrences of the day. Is God thus forward to do us good, and shall we be backward and remiss in doing him service?

4. If we attend upon God, his holy angels shall have a charge to attend upon us. They are all appointed to be ministering spirits, to minister for the good of them that shall be heirs of salvation, and more good offices they do us every day than we are aware of. What an honor, what a privilege is it to be waited on by holy angels; to be borne up in their arms, to be surrounded by their tents, what a security is the ministration of those good

spirits, against the malice of evil spirits? This honor have all they that wait on God all the day.

5. This life of communion with God, and constant attendance upon him, is a heaven upon earth. It is doing the work of heaven, and the will of God, as they do it that are in heaven; whose business it is always to behold the face of our Father. It is an earnest of the blessedness of heaven, it is a preparative for it, and a preludium to it; it is having our conversation in heaven, from whence we look for the Saviour. Looking for him as our Saviour, we look to him as our Director; and by this we make it appear, that our hearts are there, which will give us good ground to expect that we shall be there shortly.

Thirdly, Let me close with some directions, what you must do, that you may thus wait on God all the day.

1. See much of God in every creature, of his wisdom and power in the making and placing of it, and of his goodness in its serviceableness to us. Look about you, and see what a variety of wonders, what an abundance of comforts you are surrounded with; and let them all lead you to him, who is the fountain of being, and the giver of all good; all our springs are in him, and from him are all our streams; this will engage us to wait on him,

since every creature is that to us, that he makes it to be. Thus the same things which draw a carnal heart from God, will lead a gracious soul to him; and since all his works praise him, his saints will from hence take continual occasion to bless him.

It was (they say) the custom of the pious Jews of old, whatever delight they took in any creature, to give to God the glory of it; when they smelled a flower, they said, blessed be he that made this flower sweet; if they eat a morsel of bread, blessed be he that appointed bread to strengthen man's heart. If thus we taste in everything that the Lord is gracious, and suck all satisfaction from the breasts of his bounty, (and some derive his name from *Mamma*) we shall thereby be engaged constantly to depend on him, as the child is said to hang on the mother's breast.

2. See every creature to be nothing without God; the more we discern of the vanity and emptiness of the world, and all our enjoyments in it, and their utter insufficiency to make us happy, the closer we shall cleave to God, and the more intimately we shall converse with him, that we may find that satisfaction in the Father of spirits, which we have in vain sought for in the things of sense. What folly is it to make our court to the creatures, and to dance attendance at their door, whence we are sure

to be sent away empty, when we have the
Creator himself to go to, who is rich in mercy
to all that call upon him, is full, and free, and
faithful.   What can we expect from lying vanities?   Why then should we observe them, and
neglect our own mercies?   Why should we
trust to broken reeds, when we have a rock of
ages, to be the foundation of our hopes?   And
why should we draw from broken cisterns,
when we have the God of all consolation to be
the foundation of our joys.

3. Live by faith in the Lord Jesus Christ.
We cannot with any confidence wait upon God,
but in and through a Mediator, for it is by his
Son that God speaks to us, and hears from us:
all that passeth between a just God and poor
sinners, must pass through the hands of that
blessed days-man, who has laid his hand upon
them both; every prayer passeth from us to
God, and every mercy from God to us by that
hand; it is in the face of the anointed, that
God looks upon us; and in the face of Jesus
Christ, that we behold the glory and grace of
God shining; it is by Christ that we have access to God, and success with him in prayer,
and therefore must make mention of his righteousness, even of his only; and in that habitual attendance we must be all the day living
upon God, we must have an habitual dependence on him, who always appears in the pres-

ence of God for us; always gives attendance to be ready to introduce us.

4. Be frequent and serious in pious ejaculations. In waiting upon God we must often speak to him, must take all occasions to speak to him; and when we have not opportunity for a solemn address to him, he will accept of a sudden address, if it come from an honest heart. In these David waited on God all day, as appears by *ver*. 1, Unto thee, O Lord, do I lift up my soul: to thee do I dart it, and all its gracious breathings after thee. We should in a holy ejaculation ask pardon for this sin, strength against this corruption, victory over this temptation, and it shall not be in vain. This is to pray always and without ceasing; it is not the length or language of the prayer that God looks at, but the sincerity of the heart in it: and that shall be accepted, though the prayer be very short, and the groanings such as cannot be uttered.

5. Look upon every day, as those who know not but it may be your last day. At such an hour as we think not, the Son of Man comes; and therefore we cannot any morning be sure, that we shall live till night, we hear of many lately that have been snatched away very suddenly, what manner of persons therefore ought we to be in all holy conversation and godliness. Though we cannot say, we ought to

live as if we were sure this day would be our
last, yet it is certain, we ought to live as those
who do not know but it may be so; and the
rather, because we know the day of the Lord
will come first or last; and therefore we are
concerned to wait on him. For on whom
should poor dying creatures wait, but on a living God.

Death will bring us all to God, to be judged
by him; it will bring all the saints to him, to
to the vision and fruition of him; and one we
are hastening to, and hope to be forever with,
we are concerned to wait upon, and to culti-
vate an acquaintance with. Did we think
more of death, we would converse more with
God; our dying daily, is a good reason for our
worshipping daily; and therefore wherever we
are, we are concerned to keep near to God, because we know not where death will meet us:
this will alter the property of death; Enoch,
that walked with God, was translated that he
should not see death; and this will furnish us
with that which will stand us instead on the
other side death and the grave. If we continue waiting on God every day, and all the day
long, we shall grow more experienced, and consequently more expert in the great mystery of
communion with God, and thus our last days
will become our best days, our last works our
best works, and our last comforts our sweetest

comforts : in consideration of which take the prophet's advice ; Hos. xii. 6, Turn thou to thy God ; keep mercy and judgment, and wait on thy God continually.

DISCOURSE III

SHOWING

HOW TO CLOSE THE DAY WITH GOD

I will both lay me down in Peace, and sleep: for thou,
Lord, only makest me dwell in safety.—PSALM iv. 8

THIS may be understood either figuratively,
of the repose of the soul in the assurances of
God's grace ; or literally, of the repose of the
body under the protection of his providence ; I
love to give scripture its full latitude, and therefore alike in both.

1. The Psalmist having given the preference
to God's favor above any good, having chosen
that, and portioned himself in that, here expresseth his great complacency in the choice
he had made ; while he saw many making
themselves perpetually uneasy with that fruitless inquiry, Who will show us any good ?
Wearying themselves for very vanity ; he had
made himself perfectly easy by casting himself
on the divine good will, Lord, lift thou up the
light of thy countenance upon us : any good,
short of God's favor, will not serve our turn,

but that is enough, without the world's smiles: the moon and stars, and all the fires and candles in the world, will not make day without the sun; but the sun will make day without any of them. These are David's sentiments, and all the saints agree with him: finding no rest therefore, like Noah's dove in the deluged defiled world, he flies to the ark, that type of Christ, return unto thy rest, unto thy Noah, so the word is in the original, for Noah's name signifies rest, O my soul, Psal. cxvi. 7.

If God lift up the light of his countenance upon us, as it fills us with a holy joy, it puts gladness into the heart more than they have whose corn and wine increaseth, ver. 7, so it fixeth us in a holy rest, I will now lay me down and sleep. God is my God, and I am pleased, I am satisfied, I look no further, I desire no more, I dwell in safety: Or in confidence; while I walk in the light of the Lord, as I want no good, nor am sensible of any deficiency, so I fear no evil, nor am apprehensive of any danger. The Lord God is to me both a sun and a shield; a sun to enlighten and comfort me, a shield to protect and defend me.

Hence learn, that those who have the assurances of God's favor towards them, may enjoy and should labor after, a holy serenity, and security of mind. We have both these put together in that precious promise, Isa. xxxii. 17.

But the work of righteousness shall be peace, there is a present satisfaction in doing good; and in the issue, the effect of righteousness shall be quietness and assurance forever; quiet-ness in the enjoyment of good, and assurance in a freedom from evil.

1. A holy serenity is one blessed fruit of God's favor; I will now lay me down in peace and sleep. While we are under God's displea-sure, or in doubt concerning his favor, how can we have any enjoyment of ourselves! while this great concern is unsettled, the soul cannot but be unsatisfied. Hath God a controversy with thee? Give not sleep to thine eyes, nor slumber to thine eyelids, until thou hast got the controversy taken up; Go humble thyself, and make sure thy friend, thy best friend, Prov. vi. 34, and when thou hast made thy peace with him, and hast some comfortable evidence that thou art accepted of him, then say wisely and justly, what that carnal world-ling said foolishly, and without ground, Soul take thy ease, for in God, and in the covenant of grace, thou hast goods laid up for many years, goods laid up for eternity, Luke xii. 19. Are thy sins pardoned? Hast thou an interest in Christ's mediation? Doth God now in him accept thy works? Go thy way, eat thy bread with joy, and drink thy wine with a merry

heart, Eccl. ix. 7. Let this still every storm
and command, and create a calm in thy soul.

Having God to be our God in covenant, we
have enough, we have all ; and though the gracious soul still desires more of God, it never desires more than God ; in him it reposeth itself
with a perfect complacency; in him it is at
home, it is at rest, if we be but satisfied of his
loving kindness, we may be satisfied with his
loving kindness; abundantly satisfied : There
is enough in this to satiate the weary soul,
and to replenish every sorrowful soul, Jer. xxxi.
25, to fill even the hungry with good things,
with the best things ; and being filled, they
should be at rest, at rest forever, and their sleep
here should be sweet.

2. A holy security is another blessed fruit of
God's favor. Thou, Lord, makest me to dwell
in safety ; when the light of thy countenance
shines upon me I am safe, and I know I am
so, and am therefore easy, for with thy favor
wilt thou compass me as with a shield, Psal.
v. 12. Being taken under the protection of
the divine favor. Though an host of enemies
should encamp against me, yet my heart shall
not fear, in this I will be confident, Psal. xxvii.
3. Whatever God has promised me, I can
promise myself, and that is enough to indem-
nify me, and save me harmless, whatever difficulties and dangers I may meet with in the way

of my duty. Though the earth be removed, yet will not we fear, Psal. xlvi. 2, not fear any evil, no not in the valley of the shadow of death, in the territories of the king of terrors himself, for there thou art with me, thy rod and thy staff they comfort me. What the rich man's wealth is to him, in his own conceit, a strong city, and a high wall, that the good man's God is to him, Prov. xviii. 10, 11. The Almighty shall be thy gold, thy defence, Job xxii. 25.

Nothing is more dangerous than security in a sinful way, and men's crying peace, peace, to themselves, while they continue under the reigning power of a vain and carnal mind: O that the sinners that are at ease were made to tremble : nothing is more foolish than a security built upon the world, and its promises, for they are all vanity and a lie ; but nothing more reasonable in itself, or more advantageous to us, than for good people to build with assurance upon the promises of a good God, for those that keep in the way of duty, to be quiet from the fear of evil ; as those that know no evil shall befall them, no real evil, no evil, but what shall be made to work for their good; as those that know, while they continue in the allegiance to God as their king, they are under his protection, under the protection of Omnipotence itself, which enables them to bid defiance to all

malignant powers; If God be for us, who can
be against us? This security even the heathen looked upon every honest virtuous man
to be entitled to, that is *Integer vitæ sceleris-
que purus*, and thought if the world should
fall in pieces about his ears, he needed not fear
being lost in the desolations of it, *Et si frac-
tus illabatur orbis, Impavidum ferient ruinæ;*
much more reason have Christians, that hold
fast their integrity, to lay claim to it, for who
is he, or what is it, that shall harm us, if we
be followers of him that is good, in his goodness?

Now, (1.) It is the privilege of good people,
that they may be thus easy and satisfied : This
holy serenity and security of mind is allowed
them, God gives them leave to be cheerful ;
nay, it is promised them, God will speak peace
to his people, and to his saints ; he will fill
them with joy and peace in believing ; his
peace shall keep their hearts and minds ; keep
them safe, keep them calm. Nay, there is a
method appointed for their obtaining this promised serenity and security. The scriptures are
written to them that their joy may be full, and
that through patience and comfort of them they
may have hope. Ordinances are instituted to
be wells of salvation, out of which they may
draw water with joy. Ministers are ordained
to be their comforters, and the helpers of their
joy. Thus willing has God been to show to

the heirs of promise the immutability of his counsel, that they might have strong consolation, Heb. vi. 17, 18.

(2.) It is the duty of good people to labor after this holy security and serenity of mind, and to use the means appointed for the obtaining of it. Give not way to the disquieting suggestions of Satan, and to those tormenting doubts and fears that arise in your own souls. Study to be quiet, chide yourselves for your distrusts, charge yourselves to believe, and to hope in God, that you shall praise him. You are in the dark concerning yourselves, do as Paul's mariners did, cast anchor, and wish for the day. Poor trembling Christian, that art tossed with tempests, and not comforted, try to lay thee down in peace and sleep ; compose thyself into a sedate and even frame; in the name of him whom winds and seas obey, command down thy tumultuous thoughts, and say, Peace, be still ; lay that aching trembling head of thine where the beloved disciple laid his, in the bosom of the Lord Jesus ; or, if thou hast not yet attained such boldness of access to him, lay that aching trembling head of thine at the feet of the Lord Jesus, by an entire submission and resignation to him, saying, If I perish, I will perish here ; put it into his hand by an entire confidence in him ; submit it to his operation and disposal, who knows how to speak to

the heart. And if thou art not yet entered
into the sabbatism, as the word is, Heb. iv. 9,
this present rest that remaineth for the people
of God, yet look upon it to be a land of promise, and therefore though it tarry, wait for it,
for the vision is for an appointed time, and at
the end it shall speak, and shall not lie. Light
is sown for the righteous, and what is sown
shall come up again at last in a harvest of
joy.

2. The Psalmist having done his day's work,
and perhaps fatigued himself with it, it being
now bed-time, and he having given good advice
to those to whom he had wished a good night,
to commune with their own hearts upon their
beds, and to offer the evening sacrifices of
righteousness, *ver.* 4, 5, now retires to his chamber with this word, I will lay me down in peace
and sleep. That which I chose this text for,
will lead me to understand it literally, as the
disciples understood their Master, when he said,
Lazarus sleepeth, of taking rest in sleep, John
xi. 12, 13. And so we have here David's pious
thought when he was going to bed : As when
he awakes he is still with God, he is still so
when he goes to sleep, and concludes the day,
as he opened it, with meditations on God, and
sweet communion with him.

It should seem David penned this Psalm
when he was distressed and persecuted by his

enemies; perhaps it was penned on the same
occasion with the foregoing Psalm, when he
fled from Absalom his son; without were fight-
ings, and then no wonder that within were
fears; yet then he puts such a confidence in
God's protection, that he will go to bed at his
usual time, and with his usual quietness and
cheerfulness, will compose himself as at other
times; He knows his enemies have no power
against him, but what is given them from
above, and they shall have no power given
them, but what is still under the divine check
and restraint; nor shall their power be per-
mitted to exert itself so far as to do him any
real mischief, and therefore he retires into the
secret place of the Most High, and abides under
the shadow of the Almighty, and is very quiet
in his own mind. That will break a worldly
man's heart, which will not break a godly
man's sleep: Let them do their worst, saith
David, I will lay me down and sleep; the will
of the Lord be done. Now observe here,

1. His confidence in God: Thou, Lord, makest me to dwell in safety; not only makest
me safe, but makest me to know that I am so;
makest me to dwell with a good assurance: It
is the same word that is used concerning him
that walks uprightly, that he walks surely, Prov.
x. 9. He goes boldly in his way, so David here
goes boldly to his bed. He doth not carelessly

as the man of Laish, Judg. xviii. 7, but dwells at ease in God, as the sons of Zion, in the city of their solemnities, when their eyes see it a quiet habitation, Isa. xxxiii. 20.

There is one word in this part of the text that is observable; thou, Lord, only dost secure me. Some refer it to David; even when I am alone, have none of my privy-counsellors about me to advise me, none of my life-guards to fight for me, yet I am under no apprehension of danger, while God is with me. The Son of David comforted himself with this, that when all his disciples forsook him, and left him alone, yet he was not alone, for the Father was with him. Some weak people are afraid of being alone, especially in the dark, but a firm belief of God's presence with us in all places, and that divine protection which all good people are under, would silence those fears, and make us ashamed of them. Nay, our being alone a peculiar people whom God hath set apart, for himself, (as it is here, *ver.* 3.) will be our security. A sober singularity will be our safety and satisfaction, as Noah's was in the old world; Israel is a people that shall dwell alone, and not to be reckoned among the nations, and therefore may set them all at defiance, till they foolishly mingle themselves among them, Numb. xxiii. 9. Israel shall then dwell in safety alone, Deut. xxxiii. 28. The more we dwell alone,

the more safe we dwell. But our translation
refers it to God ; thou alone makest me to dwell
safely. It is done by thee only! God in pro-
tecting his people needs not any assistance,
though he sometimes makes use of instruments :
The earth helped the woman, yet he can do it
without them ; and when all other refuges
fail, his own arm works salvation ; so the Lord
alone did lead him, and there was no strange God
with him, Deut. xxxiii. 12, yet that is not all, I
depend on thee only to do it; therefore I am
easy, and think myself safe, not because I have
hosts on my side, but purely because I have
the Lord of hosts on my side.

Thou makest me to dwell in safety; That
may look either backward or forward, or rather
both : Thou hast made me to dwell in safety all
day, so that the sun has not smitten me by
day; and then it is the language of his thankfulness of the mercies he had received ; or, thou
wilt make me to dwell in safety all night, that
the moon shall not smite me by night : And
then it is the language of his dependence upon
God for further mercies ; and both these should
go together ; and our eye must be to God as
ever the same, who was, and is, and is to come ;
who hath delivered, and doth, and will.

2. His composedness in himself inferred from
hence, I will both lay me down and sleep: *Simul*
or *pariter in pace cubabo.* They that have

their corn and wine increasing, that have
abundance of the wealth and pleasure of this
world, they lay them down and sleep content-
edly, as Boaz at the end of the heap of corn,
Ruth iii. 7. But though I have not what they
have, I can lay me down in peace and sleep,
as well as they. We make it to join, his lying
down and his sleeping ; I will not only lay me
down, as one that desires to be composed, but
will sleep as one that really is so.   Some make
it to intimate his falling asleep presently after
he had laid him down; so well wearied was
he with the work of the day, and so free from
any of those disquieting thoughts which would
keep him from sleeping.

Now these are words put into our mouths,
with which to compose ourselves when we
retire at night to our repose ; and we should
take care so to manage ourselves all day,
especially when it draws towards night, as that
we may not be disfitted, and put out of frame,
for our evening devotions ; that our hearts may
not be overcharged either on the one hand
with surfeiting and drunkenness, as theirs
often are that are men of pleasure ; or on the
other hand with the cares of this life, as theirs
often are that are men of business ; but that
we may have such a command both of our
thought, and of our time, as that we may finish
our daily work well ; which will be an earnest

of our finishing our life's work well; and all is
well indeed that ends everlastingly well.

Doct. As we must begin the day with God,
   and wait upon him all the day, so we
   must endeavor to close it with him.

This duty of closing the day with God, and
in a good frame, I know not how better to open
to you, than by going over the particulars in
the text, in their order; and recommending to
you David's example.

First. Let us retire to lay us down; nature
calls for rest as well as food : man goes forth to
his work and labor, and goes to and fro about
it, but it is only till evening, and then it is time
to lie down.   We read of Ishbosheth, that he
lay on his bed at noon, but death met him
there, 2 Sam. iv. 5, 6. and of David himself,
that he came off from his bed at evening-tide,
but sin, a worse thing than death, met him
there, 2 Sam. xi. 2.   We must work the works
of him that sent us while it is day, it will be
time enough to lie down when the night comes;
and no man can work; and it is then proper
and seasonable to lie down : it is promised,
Zeph. ii. 7. They shall lie down in the evening, and with that promise we must comply,
and rest in the time appointed for rest; and

not turn day into night, and night into day, as many do upon some ill account or other.

1. Some sit up to do mischief to their neighbors ; to kill, and steal, and to destroy; in the dark they dig through houses, which they had marked for themselves in the day time, Job xxiv. 16. David complains of his enemies, that at evening they go round about the city, Psal. lix. 6. They that do evil hate the light. Judas the traitor was in quest of his Master, with his band of men, when he should have been in his bed. And it is an aggravation of the wickedness of the wicked when they take so much pains to compass an ill design, and have their hearts so much upon it, that they sleep not except they have done mischief, Prov. iv. 16. As it is a shame to those who profess to make it their business to do good, that they cannot find in their hearts to intrench upon any of their gratifications of sense in pursuance of it ;

Ut jugulent Homines, surgunt de nocte Latrones,
Tuque ut te serves non expergisceris ?

say then, while others sit up watching for an opportunity to be mischievous, I will lay me down and be quiet, and do nobody any harm.

2. Others sit up in pursuit of the world, and the wealth of it. They not only rise up early, but they sit up late, in the eager prosecution of their covetous practices, Psal. cxxvii. 2, and

either to get or save, deny themselves their most necessary sleep; and this their way is their folly, for hereby they deprive themselves of the comfortable enjoyment of what they have, which is the end, under pretence of care and pains to obtain more, which is but the means. Solomon speaks of those that neither day nor night sleep with their eyes, Eccl. viii. 16, that make themselves perfect slaves, and drudges to the world, than which there is not a more cruel task-master : and thus they make that which of itself is vanity, to be to them vexation of spirit, for they weary themselves for every vanity, Heb. ii. 13, and are so miserably in love with their chain, that they deny themselves not only the spiritual rest God has provided for them as the God of grace, but the natural rest, which, as the God of nature, he has provided, and is a specimen of the wrong sinners do to their own bodies, as well as to their own souls. Let us see the folly of it, and never labor thus for the meat that perisheth, and that abundance of the rich which will not suffer him to sleep; but let us labor for that meat which endureth to eternal life, that grace which is the earnest of glory, the abundance of which will make our sleep sweet to us.

3. Others sit up in the indulgence of their pleasures; they will not lay them down in due time, because they cannot find in their hearts

to leave their vain sports and pastimes, their
music, and dancing, and plays, their cards and
dice ; or which is worse, their rioting and ex-
cess, for they that are drunk are drunk in the
night. It is bad enough when these gratifications of a base lust, or at least of a vain mind,
are suffered to devour the whole evening, and
then to engross the whole soul, as they are apt
enough to do insensibly ; so that there is neither
time nor heart for the evening-devotions, either
in the closet or in the family ; but it is much
worse when they are suffered to go far into the
night too, for then of course they trespass upon
the ensuing morning, and steal away the time
that should then also be bestowed upon the exercises of religion. Those that can of choice,
and with so much pleasure sit up till I know
not what time of night, to make, as they say,
a merry night of it, to spend their time in fil-
thiness, and foolish talking and jesting which
are not convenient, would think themselves
hardly dealt with, if they should be kept one
half hour past their sleeping time, engaged in
any good duties, and would have called blessed
Paul himself a long-winded preacher, and have
censured him as very indiscreet, when, upon a
particular occasion he continued his speech till
midnight, Acts xx. 7. And how loth would
they be with David at midnight, to rise and

give thanks to God : or with their Master to continue all night in prayer to God.

Let the corrupt affections, which run out thus and trangress be mortified, and not gratified; those that have allowed themselves in such irregularities ; if they have allowed themselves an impartial reflection, cannot but have found the inconvenience of them, and that they have been a prejudice to the prosperity of the soul, and should therefore deny themselves for their own good. One rule for the closing of the day well, is to keep good hours : everything is beautiful in its season. I have heard it said long since, and I beg leave to repeat it now, that

> Early to bed and early to rise,
> Is the way to be healthy, and wealthy, and wise.

We shall now take it for granted, that unless some necessary business, or some work of mercy, or some more than ordinary act of devotion, keep you up beyond your usual time ; you are disposed to lay you down. And let us lay us down with thankfulness to God, and with thoughts of dying ; with penitent reflections upon the sins of the day ; and with humble supplications for the mercies of the night.

1. Let us lie down with thankfulness to God. When we retire to our bed-chambers or closets, we should lift up our hearts to God,

the God of our mercies, and make him the God of our praises whenever we go to bed. I am sure we do not want matter for praise, if we do not want a heart. Let us therefore address ourselves then to that pleasant duty, that work which is its own wages. The evening sacrifice was to be a sacrifice of praise.

(1.) We have reason to be thankful for the many mercies of the day past, which we ought particularly to review, and to say, blessed be the Lord who daily loadeth us with his benefits. Observe the constant series of mercies, which has not been interrupted, or broken in upon any day. Observe the particular instances of mercy with which some days have been signalized and made remarkable. It is he that has granted us life and favor, it is his visitation that preserves our spirits. Think how many are the calamities we are every day preserved from ; the calamities which we are sensibly exposed to, and perhaps have been delivered from the imminent danger of; and those which we have not been apprehensive of; many which we have deserved, and which others, better than we are, groan under. All our bones have reason to say, Lord, who is like unto thee ? For it is God that keepeth all our bones, not one of them is broken : It is of his mercies that we are not consumed.

Think how many are the comforts we are

every day surrounded with, all which we are
indebted to the bounty of the divine providence
for ; every bit we eat, and every drop we drink
is mercy; every step we take, and every breath
we draw, mercy. All the satisfaction we have
in the agreeableness and affections of our relations, and in the society and serviceableness of
our friends : All the success we have in our
callings and employments, and the pleasure
we take in them : All the joy which Zebulun
has in his going out, and Issachar in his tents,
is what we have reason to acknowledge with
thankfulness to God's praise.

Yet it is likely the day has not passed without some cross accidents, something or other
has afflicted and disappointed us, and if it has,
yet that must not indispose us for praise ; however it be, yet God is good ; and it is our duty
in everything to give thanks, and to bless the
name of the Lord when he takes away, as well
as when he gives ; for our afflictions are but
few, and a thousand times deserved ; our mercies are many, and a thousand times forfeited.

(2.) We have reason to be thankful for the
shadows of the evening, which call us to retire
and lie down. The same wisdom, power and
goodness that makes the morning, makes the
evening also to rejoice ; and gives us cause to be
thankful for the drawing of the curtains of the
night about us in favor to our repose, as well

as for the opening of the eyelids of the morning upon us in favor to our business. When God divided between the light and the darkness, and allotted to both of them their time successively, he saw that it was good it should be so; in a world of mixtures and changes, nothing more proper. Let us therefore give thanks to that God who forms the light, and creates the darkness; and believe, that as in the revolutions of time, so in the revolutions of the events of time, the darkness of affliction may be as needful for us in its season, as the light of prosperity. If the hireling longs till the shadow comes, let him be thankful for it when it doth come, that the burthen and the heat of the day is not perpetual.

(3.) We have reason to be thankful for a quiet habitation to lie down in; that we are not driven out from among men as Nebuchadnezzar, to lie down with the beasts of the field; that though we were born like the wild ass's colt, yet we have not with the wild ass the wilderness for our habitation, and the desolate and barren land for our dwelling. That we are not to wander in deserts and mountains, in dens and caves of the earth, as many of God's dear saints and servants have been forced to do, of whom the world was not worthy; But the good Shepherd makes us lie down in green pastures: That we have not, as Jacob, the cold ground for our bed, and a stone for our pillow, which yet one would be content with, and covet, if with it one could have his dream.

(4.) We have reason to be thankful that we are not forced to sit up; that our Master not only gives us leave to lie down, but orders that nothing shall prevent our lying down. Many go to bed, but cannot lie down there, by reason of painful and languishing sicknesses, of that nature, that if they lie down they cannot breathe: Our bodies are of the same mould, and it is of the Lord's mercies that we are not so afflicted. Many are kept up by sickness in their families; children are ill, and they must attend them: If God takes sickness away from the midst of us, and keeps it away, so that no plague comes near our dwellings, a numerous family perhaps, and all well, it is a mercy we are bound to be very thankful for, and to value in proportion to the greatness of the affliction, where sickness prevails. Many are kept up by the fear of enemies, of soldiers, of thieves; The goodman of the house watcheth, that his house may not be broken through: but our lying down is not prevented or disturbed by the alarms of war, we are delivered from the noise of archers in the places of repose; therefore should we rehearse the righteous acts of the Lord, even his righteous acts towards the inhabitants of his villages in Israel, which under his protection are as safe as walled cities with gates and bars. When we lie down, let us thank God that we may lie down.

2. Let us lie down with thoughts of death, and of that great change which at death we must pass under. The conclusion of every day should put us in mind of the conclusion of all our days; when our night comes, our long night, which will put a period to our work, and bring the honest laborer, both to take his rest, and receive his penny. It is good for us to think frequently of dying, to think of it as oft as we go to bed ; it will help to mortify the corruptions of our own hearts, which are our daily burthens, to arm us against the temptations of the world, which are our daily snares ; it will wean us from our daily comforts, and make us easy under our daily crosses and fatigues. It is good for us to think familiarly of dying, to think of it as our going to bed, that by thinking often of it, and thinking thus of it, we may get above the fear of it.

(1.) At death we shall retire, as we do at bed-time ; we shall go to be private for a while, till the public appearance at the great day ; Man lyeth down, and riseth not till the heavens be no more ; till then they shall not awake, nor be raised out of their sleep, Job xiv. 12. Now we go abroad to see and be seen and to no higher purpose do some spend their day, spend their life; but when death comes, there is an end of both; we shall then see no more in this world, I shall behold man no more: Isa. xxxviii. 11, we shall then be seen no more; the eye of him that hath seen me, shall see me no more; Job vii. 8, we shall be hid in the grave, and cut off from all living. To die is to bid good night to all our friends, to put a period to our conversation with them; we bid them farewell, but blessed be God, it is not an eternal farewell. We hope to meet them again in the morning of the resurrection, to part no more.

2. At death we shall put off the body, as we put off our clothes when we lie down. The soul is the man, the body is but clothes; at death we shall be unclothed, the earthly house of this tabernacle shall be dissolved, the garment of the body shall be laid aside; death strips us, and sends us naked out of the world, as we came into it; strips the soul of all the disguises wherein it appeared before men, that it may appear naked and open before God. Our grave clothes are night clothes.

When we are weary and hot, our clothes are a burthen, and we are very willing to throw them off, are not easy till we are undressed: thus we that are in this tabernacle do groan being burthened; but when death frees the soul from the load and incumbrance of the body, which hinders its repose in its spiritual satisfactions, how easy it will be ? Let us think then of putting off the body at death, with as much pleasure as we do of putting off our clothes at night ; be as loose to them as we are to our clothes ; and comfort ourselves with this thought ; that though we are unclothed at death, if we be clothed with Christ and his grace, we shall not be found naked, but be clothed upon with immortality. We have new clothes a making, which shall be ready to put on next morning ; a glorious body like Christ's, instead of a vile body like the beasts.

(3.) At death we shall lie down in the grave as our body shall lie down in the dust: Job xx. 11. To those that die in sin, and impenitent, the grave is a dungeon, their iniquities which are upon their bones, and which lie down with them, make it so; but to those that die in Christ, that die in faith, it is a bed, a bed of rest, where there is no tossings to and fro until the dawning of the day, as sometimes there are upon the easiest beds we have in this world ; where there is no danger of being scared with dreams, and terrified with visions of the night ; there is no being chastened with pain on that bed, or the multitude of the bones with strong pain. It is the privilege of those, who while they live walk in their uprightness, that when they die they enter into peace, and rest in their beds, Isa. lvii. 2. Holy Job comforts himself with this, in the midst of his agonies, that he shall shortly make his bed in the darkness, and be easy there. It is a bed of roses, a bed of spices to all believers ever since he lay in it, who is the rose of Sharon, and the lily of the valleys.

Say then of thy grave, as thou dost of thy bed at night, there the weary are at rest; with this further consolation, that thou shalt not only rest there, but rise thence shortly, abundantly refreshed; shalt be called up to meet the beloved of thy soul, and to be forever with him : shalt rise to a day which will not renew thy cares, as every day on earth doth, but secure to thee unmixed and everlasting joys. How comfortably may we lie down at night, if such thoughts as these lie down with us ? And how comfortably may we lie down at death, if we have accustomed ourselves to such thoughts as these.

3. Let us lie down with penitent reflections upon the sins of the day past. Praising God and delighting ourselves in him is such pleasant work, and so much the work of angels, that methinks it is pity we should have anything else to do; but the truth is, we make other work for ourselves by our own folly, that is not so pleasant, but absolutely needful, and that is repentance. While we are at night solacing

ourselves in God's goodness, yet we must inter-
mix therewith the afflicting of ourselves for our
own baldness; both must have their place in
us, and they will very well agree together; for
we must take our work before us.

(1.) We must be convinced of it, that we
are still contracting guilt; we carry corrupt
natures about with us, which are bitter roots
that bear gall and wormwood, and all we say
or do is imbittered by them. In many things
we all offend, insomuch that there is not a just
man upon earth that doth good and sins not.
We are in the midst of a defiling world, and
cannot keep ourselves perfectly unspotted from
it. If we say we have no sin, or that we have
past a day and have not sinned, we deceive
ourselves; for if we know the truth by ourselves, we shall see cause to cry, Who can
understand his errors? Cleanse us from our
secret faults; faults which we ourselves are
not aware of. We ought to aim at a sinless
perfection, with as strict a watchfulness as if
we could attain it: But after all must acknowledge, that we come short of it; that we have
not yet attained, neither are already perfect.
We find it by constant sad experience, for it is
certain we do enough every day to bring us
upon our knees at night.

(2.) We must examine our consciences, that
we may find out our particular transgressions

the day past. Let us every night search and
try our ways, our thoughts, words, and actions,
compare them with the rule of the word, look
our faces in that glass, that we may see our
spots and may be particular in the acknowledgment of them. It will be good for us to ask,
What have we done this day ? What have we
done amiss ? What duty have we neglected ?
What false step have we taken ? How have
we carried it in our callings, in our converse?
Have we done the duties of our particular relations, and accommodated ourselves to the will
of God in every event of providence. By doing this frequently, we shall grow in our acquaintance with ourselves, than which nothing
will contribute more to our soul's prosperity.

(3.) We must renew our repentance for whatever we find has been amiss in us, or has been
said or done amiss by us. We must be sorry for
it, and sadly lament it, and take shame to
ourselves for it, and give glory to God by making confession. If anything appear to have
been wrong more than ordinary, that must be
particularly bewailed ; and in general, we must
be mortified for our sins of daily infirmity,
which we ought not to think slightly of, because
they are returning daily, but rather be the
more ashamed of them, and of that fountain
within which casts out these waters.

It is good to be speedy in renewing our

repentance; before the heart be hardened by
the deceitfulness of sin.   Delays are dangerous;
green wounds may soon be cured, if taken in
time, but if they stink and are corrupt, as the
Psalmist complains, Psal. xxxviii. 5, it is our
fault and folly, and the cure will be difficult.
Though through the weakness of the flesh we
fall into sin daily, if we get up again by renewed
repentance at night, we are not, nor ought we
to think ourselves utterly cast down.   The sin
that humbles us shall not ruin us.

(4.) We must make a fresh application of the
blood of Christ to our souls for the remission
of our sins, and the gracious acceptance of our
repentance.   We must not think that we have
need of Christ only at our first conversion to
God; No, we have daily need of him, as our
advocate with the Father, and therefore as
such he always appears in the presence of God
for us, and attends continually to this very
thing.   Even our sins of daily infirmity would
be our ruin, if he had not made satisfaction for
them, and did not still make intercession for us.
He that is washed, still needeth to wash his
feet from the filth he contracts in every step;
and blessed be God, there is a fountain opened
for us to wash in, and it is always open.

(5.) We must apply ourselves to the throne
of grace for peace and pardon.   Those that
repent must pray, that the thought of their

heart may be forgiven them, Acts viii. 22.　And it is good to be particular in our prayers for the pardon of sin; that as Hannah said concerning Samuel, for this child I prayed; so we may be able to say, for the forgiveness of this I prayed. However, the publican's prayer in general, is a very proper one for each of us to lie down with, God be merciful to me a sinner.

4. Let us lie down with humble supplications for the mercies of the night.　Prayer is as necessary in the evening, as it was in the morning, for we have the same need of the divine favor and care, to make the evening outgoings to rejoice, that we had to beautify those of the morning.

(1.) We must pray, that our outward man may be under the care of God's holy angels, who are the ministers of his providence.　God hath promised, that he will give his angels charge concerning those who make the Most High their refuge, and that they shall pitch their tents round about them and deliver them; and what he hath promised, we may and must pray for; not as if God needed the service of the angels, or as if he did himself quit all the care of his people, and turn it over to them: But it appears by abundance of scripture proofs, that they are employed about the people of God, whom he takes under his special protection, though they are not seen both for

the honor of God by whom they are charged,
and for the honor of the saints with whom
they are charged. It was the glory of Solomon's bed, that threescore valiant men were
about it, of the valiant of Israel, all holding
swords, because of fear in the night, Cant. iii.
7, 8. But much more honorably and comfortably are all true believers attended, for though
they lie never so meanly, they have hosts of
angels surrounding their beds, and by the ministration of good spirits, are preserved from
malignant spirits. But God will for this be
inquired of by the house of Israel; Christ
himself must pray the Father, and he will
send to his relief legions of angels, Matth.
xxvi. 53. Much more reason have we to ask,
that it may be given us.

(2.) We must pray, that our inward man
may be under the influences of his Holy Spirit,
who is the Author and fountain of his grace.
As public ordinances are opportunities in which
the Spirit works upon the hearts of men, and
therefore when we attend on them, we must
pray for the Spirit's operations, so are private
retirements, and therefore we must put up the
same prayer, when we enter upon them. We
find, that in slumberings upon the bed, God
openeth the ears of men, and sealeth their instruction, Job. xxxiii. 15, 16. And with this
David's experiences concur, he found that God

visited him in the night, and tried him and so discovered him to himself, Psal. xvii. 3. And that God gave him counsel, and his reins instructed him in the night season, and so he discovered himself to him, Psal. xvi. 7. He found that was a proper season for remembering God, and meditating upon him; and in order to our due improvement of this proper season for conversing with God in solitude, we need the powerful and benign influences of the blessed Spirit, which therefore when we lie down we should earnestly pray for, and humbly put ourselves under, and submit ourselves to. How God's grace may work upon us, when we are asleep we know not; the soul will act in a state of separation from the body, and how far it doth act independent on the body, when the bodily senses are all locked up we cannot say, but are sure, that the Spirit of the Lord is not bound; we have reason to pray, not only that our minds may not be either disturbed or polluted by evil dreams, in which for aught we know, evil spirits sometimes have a hand, but may be instructed and quieted by good dreams, which Plutarch reckons among the evidences of increase and proficiency in virtue, and on which the good spirit has an influence. I have heard of a good man, that used to pray at night for good dreams.

Secondly, When we lay us down, our care and endeavor must be to lay us down in peace. It is promised to Abraham, that he shall go to his grave in peace, Gen. xv. 15, and this promise is sure to all his spiritual seed, for the end of the upright man is peace; Josiah dies in peace, though he is killed in a battle; now as an earnest of this, let us every night lie down in peace. It is threatened to the wicked, that they shall lie down in sorrow, Isa. l. 11. It is promised to the righteous, that they shall lie down, and none shall make them afraid, Lev. xxvi. 6, Job xi. 19. Let us then enter into this rest, this blessed Sabbatism, and take care that we come not short of it.

1. Let us lie down in peace with God; for without this there can be no peace at all; There is no peace, saith my God, to the wicked, whom God is at war with. A state of sin is a state of enmity against God; they that continue in that state are under the wrath and curse of God, and cannot lie down in peace: What have they to do with peace? Hasten therefore, (sinner,) hasten to make thy peace with God in Jesus Christ, by repentance and faith; take hold on his strength, that thou mayest make peace with him, and thou shalt make peace, for fury is not with him. Conditions of peace are offered, consent to them; close with him who is our Peace; take Christ

upon his own terms, Christ upon any terms.
Defer not to do this ; dare not to sleep in that
condition, in which thou darest not die.   Es-
cape for thy life, look not behind thee.   Ac-
quaint now thyself with him, now presently,
and be at peace, and thereby this good shall
come unto thee, thou shalt lie down in peace.

Sin is ever and anon making mischief
between God and our souls, provoking God
against us, alienating us from God, we therefore need to be every night making peace, rec-
onciling ourselves to him and to his holy will,
by the agency of his Spirit upon upon us, and
begging of him to be reconciled to us, through
the intercession of his Son for us ; that there
may be no distance, no strangeness between
us and God, no interposing cloud to hinder his
mercies from coming down upon us, or our
prayers from coming up unto him.   Being jus-
tified by faith, we have this peace with God,
through our Lord Jesus Christ ; and then we
may not only lie down in peace ; but we rejoice in hope of the glory of God.   Let this be
our first care, that God have no quarrel with
us, nor we with him.

2. Let us lie down in peace with all men ;
we are concerned to go to sleep, as well as to
go to die in charity.   Those that converse
much with the world can scarce pass a day,
but something or other happens that is pro-

voking, some affront is given them, some injury done them, at least they so think; when
they retire at night and reflect upon it, they
are apt to magnify the offence, and while they
are musing on it the fire burns, their resent-
ments rise, and they begin to say, I will do so
to him as he has done to me, Prov. xxiv. 29.
Then is the time of ripening the passion into
a rooted malice, and meditating revenge; then
therefore let wisdom and grace be set on work,
to extinguish this fire from hell before it get
head, then let this root of bitterness be killed
and plucked up; and let the mind be disposed
to forgive the injury, and to think well of, and
wish well to him that did it.   If others incline
to quarrel with us, yet let us resolve not to
quarrel with them.   Let us resolve that whatever the affront or injury was, it shall neither
disquiet our spirits, nor make us to fret, which
Peninnah aimed at in provoking Hannah, 1
Sam. i. 6, nor sour or imbitter our spirits, or
make us peevish and spiteful: But that we
still love ourselves, and love our neighbors as
ourselves, and therefore not by harboring malice, do any wrong to ourselves or our neighbor.   And we shall find it much easier in
itself, and much more pleasant in the reflection, to forgive twenty injuries than to avenge
one.

That it should be our particular care at

night, to reconcile ourselves to those who have been injurious to us, is intimated in that charge, Eph. iv. 26. Let not the sun go down upon your wrath. If your passion has not cooled before, let it be abated by the cool of the evening, and quite disappear with the setting sun. You are then to go to bed, and if you lie down with these unmortified passions boiling in your breasts, your soul is among lions, you lie down in a bed of thorns, in a nest of scorpions. Nay, some have observed from what follows immediately, Neither give place to the devil, *ver*. 27, that those who go to bed in malice, have the devil for their bed-fellow. We cannot lie down at peace with God, unless we be at peace with men : nor in faith pray to be forgiven, unless we forgive. Let us therefore study the things that make for peace, for the peace of our own spirits, by living as much as in us lies peaceably with all men. I am for peace, yea, though they are for war.

3. Let us lie down in peace with ourselves, with our minds, with a sweet composedness of spirit and enjoyment of ourselves ; return unto thy rest, O my soul, and be easy ; let nothing disturb my soul, my darling.

But when may we lie down in peace? At night.

1. If we have by the grace of God in some

measure done the work of the day, and filled
it up with duty, we may then lie down in peace
at night. If we have the testimony of our
consciences for us, that in simplicity and godly
sincerity, not with fleshly wisdom, but by the
grace of God we have this day had our conversation in the world, that we have done some
good in our places, something that will turn to
a good account; if our hearts do not reproach
us with a *diem perdidi*, alas! I have lost a
day: or with that which is worse, the spending of that time in the service of sin, which
should have been spent in the service of God ;
but if on the contrary we have abode with God,
have been in his fear, and waited on him all
the day long, we may then lie down in peace,
for God saith, Well done, good and faithful
servant; and the sleep of the laboring man, of
the laboring Christian, is sweet, is very sweet,
when he can say, as I am a day's journey
nearer my end, so I am a day's work fitter for
it. Nothing will make our bed-chambers pleasant, and our beds easy, like the witness of the
Spirit of God with our spirits, that we are going forward for heaven ; and a conscience kept
void of offence, which will be not only a continual feast, but a continual rest.

2. If we have by faith and patience, and
submission to the divine will reconciled ourselves to all the events of the day, so as to be

uneasy at nothing that God has done, we may then lie down in peace at night. Whatever hath fallen out cross to us, it shall not fret us, but we will kiss the rod, take up the cross, and say, all is well that God doth. Thus we must in our patience keep possession of our own souls, and not suffer any affliction to put us out of the possession of them. We have met with disappointments, in husbandry perhaps, in trade, at sea, debtors prove insolvent, creditors prove severe, but this and the other proceedeth from the Lord, there is a providence in it, every creature is what God makes it to be, and therefore I am dumb, I open not my mouth : That which pleaseth God ought not to displease me.

3. If we have renewed our repentance for sin, and made a fresh application of the blood of Christ to our souls for the purifying of our consciences, we may then lay us down in peace. Nothing can break in upon our peace but sin, that is it that troubles the camp ; if that be taken away, there shall no evil befall us. The inhabitant though he be far from well, yet shall not say I am sick, shall not complain of sickness, for the people that dwell therein shall be forgiven their iniquity, Isa. xxxiii. 22. The pardon of sin has enough in it to balance all our griefs, and therefore to silence all our complaints : a man sick of the palsy, yet has reason to be easy, nay, and to be of good cheer, if

Christ saith to him, thy sins are forgiven thee, and I am thy salvation.

4. If we have put ourselves under the divine protection for the ensuing night, we may then lay us down in peace. If by faith and prayer, we have run into the name of the Lord as our strong tower, have fled to take shelter under the shadow of his wings, and made the Lord our refuge and our habitation, we may then speak peace to ourselves, for God in his word speaks peace to us. If David has an eye to the cherubims, between which God is said to dwell, when he saith, Psal. lvii. 1; In the shadow of thy wings will I make my refuge; yet certainly he has an eye to the similitude Christ makes use of, of a hen gathering her chickens under her wings, when he saith, Psal. xci. 4, He shall cover thee with his feathers, and under his wings shalt thou trust; and the chickens under the wings of the hen are not only safe, but warm and pleased.

5. If we have cast all our cares for the day following upon God, we may then lay us down in peace. Taking thought for the morrow is the great hindrance of our peace in the night; let us but learn to live without disquieting care, and to refer the issue of all events to that God who may and can do what he will, and will do what is best for those that love and fear him: Father, thy will be done, and then we

make ourselves easy. Our Saviour presseth this very much upon his disciples, not to perplex themselves with thoughts what they shall eat, and what they shall drink, and wherewithal they shall be clothed, because their heavenly Father knows that they have need of these things, and will see that they be supplied. Let us therefore ease ourselves of this burthen, by casting it on him who careth for us ; what need he care, and we care too ?

Thirdly, Having laid ourselves down in peace, we must compose ourselves to sleep. I will lay me down and sleep. The love of sleep for sleeping sake, is the character of the sluggard, but as it is nature's physic for the recruiting of its weary powers, it is to be looked upon as a mercy equal to that of our food, and in its season to be received with thankfulness.

And with such thoughts as these we may go to sleep.

1. What poor bodies are these we carry about with us, that call for rest and relief so often, that are so soon tired even with doing nothing, or next to nothing. It is an honor to man above the beasts, that he is made to go erect, *Os Homini sublime dedit,* it was part of the serpent's curse, on thy belly shalt thou go ; yet we have little reason to boast of this honor, when we observe how little a while we can stand upright, and how soon we are burthened

with our honor, and are forced to lie down. The powers of the soul, and the senses of the body, are our honor, but it is mortifying to consider how after a few hours use they are all locked up under a total disability of acting, and it is necessary they should be so. Let not the wise man glory in his wisdom, or the strong man in his strength, since they both lie for a fourth part of their time utterly bereft of strength and wisdom, and on a level with the weak and foolish.

2. What a sad thing is it to be under a necessity of losing so much precious time as we do in sleep. That we should lie so many hours every four and twenty, in no capacity at all of serving God or our neighbor, of doing any work of piety or charity. Those that consider how short our time is, and what a great deal of work we have to do, and how fast the day of account hastens on, cannot but grudge to spend so much time in sleep, cannot but wish to spend as little as may be in it; cannot but be quickened by it to redeem time when they are awake, and cannot but long to be there where there shall be no need of sleep, but they shall be as the angels of God, and never rest day or night from the blessed work of praising God.

3. What a good master do we serve, that allows us time for sleep, and furnisheth us

with conveniences for it, and makes it refreshing and reviving to us? By this it appears,
the Lord is for the body, and it is a good reason why we should present our bodies to him
as living sacrifices, and glorify him with them.
Nay, sleep is spoken of as given by promise to
the saints, Psal. cxxvii. 2, So he giveth his beloved sleep. The godly man hath the enjoyment of that in a quiet resignation to God,
which the worldly man labors in vain for, in
the eager pursuit of the world. What a differ-
ence is there between the sleep of a sinner,
that is not sensible of his being within a step
of hell, and the sleep of a saint, that has good
hopes, through grace, of his being within a
step of heaven ; that is the sleep God gives to
his beloved.

4. How piteous is the case of those from
whose eyes sleep departs, through pain of body
or anguish of mind, and to whom wearisome
nights are appointed ; who, when they lie down,
say, When shall we arise ? And who are thus
made a terror to themselves. It was said, that
of all the inhuman tortures used by those
whom the French king employed to force his
Protestant subjects to renounce their religion,
none prevailed more, than keeping them by
violence long waking. When we find how
earnestly nature craves sleep, and how much it
is refreshed by it, we should think with com-

passion of those, who, upon any account, want that and other comforts which we enjoy, and pray for them.

5. How ungrateful we have been to the God of our mercies, in suffering sleep, which is so great a support and comfort to us, to be our hindrance in that which is good. As when it has been the gratification of our sloth and laziness, when it has kept us from our hour of prayer in the morning, and disfitted us for our hour of prayer at night; or when we have slept unseasonably in the worship of God; as Eutychus when Paul was preaching; and the disciples, when Christ was in his agony at prayer. How justly might we be deprived of the comfort of sleep, and upbraided with this as the provoking cause of it; What! could ye not watch with me one hour?. Those that would sleep and cannot, must think how often they should have kept awake and would not.

6. We have now one day less to live than we had in the morning; the thread of time is winding off apace, its sands are running down, and as Time goes, Eternity comes; it is hasting on; our day's are swifter than a weaver's shuttle; which passeth and repasseth in an instant; and what do we of the work of time? What forwardness are we in to give up our account? O that we could always go to sleep with death upon our thoughts, how it would

quicken us to improve time ! It would make our sleep not the less desirable, but it would make our death much the less formidable.

6. To thy glory, O God, I now go to sleep: whether we eat, or drink, yea, or sleep, for that is included in whatever we do, we must do it to the glory of God. Why do I go to sleep now, but that my body may be fit to serve my soul, and able for a while to keep pace with it in the service of God to-morrow. Thus common actions by being directed towards our great end, are done after a godly sort, and abound to our account; and thus the advantages we have by them are sanctified to us; to the pure all things are pure; and whether we wake or sleep, we live together with Christ, 1 Thess. v. 10.

8. To thy grace, O God, and to the word of thy grace I now commend myself. It is good to fall asleep, with a fresh surrender of our whole selves, body, soul and spirit to God ; now return to God as thy rest, O my soul, for he has dealt bountifully with thee ; thus we should commit the keeping of our souls to him, falling asleep as David did, Psal. xxxi. 5, with, into thy hands I commit my spirit ; and as Stephen did, Lord Jesus receive my spirit. Sleep doth not only resemble death, but is sometimes an inlet to it : many go to sleep and never awake, but sleep the sleep of death, which is a good reason why we should go to sleep with

dying thoughts, and put ourselves under the protection of a living God, and then, sudden death will be no surprise to us.

9. O that when I awake I may be still with God; that the parenthesis of sleep, though long, may not break off the thread of my communion with God, but that as soon as I wake I may resume it. O that when I awake in the night I may have my mind turned to good thoughts, may remember God upon my bed, who then is at my right hand, and to whom the darkness and the light are both alike; and that I may sweetly meditate upon him in the night-watches; that thus even that time may be redeemed, and improved to the best advantage, which otherwise is in danger not only of being lost in vain thoughts, but misspent in ill ones. O that when I awake in the morning, my first thoughts may be of God, that with them my heart may be seasoned for all day.

10. O that I may enter into a better rest than that which I am now entering upon! the Apostle speaks of a rest, which we that have believed do enter into, even in this world, as well as of a rest which in the other world remains for the people of God, Heb. iv. 4. 9. Believers rest from sin and the world, they rest in Christ, and in God through Christ; they enjoy a satisfaction in the covenant of grace,

and their interest in that covenant; this is my rest forever, here will I dwell. They enter into this ark, and they are not only safe, but easy. Now, O that I might enjoy this rest while I live, and when I die, might enter into something more than rest, even the joy of my Lord, a fulness of joy.

Fourthly, We must do all this in a believing dependence upon God and his power, providence and grace. Therefore I lay me down in peace, and compose myself to sleep, because thou, Lord, keepest me, and assurest me that thou dost so; Thou, Lord, makest me to dwell in safety. David takes notice of God's compassing his path, and his lying down, as he observes, Psalm cxxxiv. 3. He sees his eye upon him, when he is retired into his bedchamber, and none else sees him; when he is in the dark, and none else can see him. Here he takes notice of him, compassing his lying down as his preserver; and sees his hand about him, to protect him from evil, and keep him safe; feels his hand under him to support him, and to make him easy.

1. It is by the power of God's providence that we are kept safe in the night, and on that providence we must depend continually. It is he that preserveth man and beast, Psal. xxxvi. 6, that upholds all things by the word of his power. That death, which by sin entered into

the world, would soon lay all waste, if God
did not shelter his creatures from its arrows,
which are continually flying about. We cannot but see ourselves exposed in the night.
Our bodies carry about with them the seeds of
all diseases; death is always working in us, a
little thing would stop the circulation either of
the blood or the breath, and then we are gone;
either never wake, or wake under the arrests
of death. Men by sin are exposed to one
another; many have been murdered in their
beds, and many burned in their beds. And
our greatest danger of all is from the malice of
evil spirits, that go about seeking to devour.

We are very unable to help ourselves, and
our friends unable to help us; we are not aware
of the particulars of our danger, nor can we
foresee which way it will arise; and therefore
know not where to stand upon our guard; or
if we did, we know not how. When Saul was
asleep, he lost his spear and cruse of water,
and might as easily have lost his head as Sisera
did when he was asleep, by the hand of a
woman. What poor helpless creatures are we,
and how easily are we overcome when sleep
has overcome us? Our friends are asleep too,
and cannot help us. An illness may seize us
in the night, which if they be called up and
come to us, they cannot help us against; the

most skilful and tender physicians are of no value.

It is therefore God's providence that protects us night after night, his care, his goodness. That was the hedge about Job, about him and his house, and all that he had round about, Job. i. 10, a hedge that Satan himself could not break through, nor find a gap in, though he traversed it round. There is a special protection which God's people are taken under, they are hid in his pavilion, in the secret of his tabernacle, under the protection of his promise, Psal. xxvii. 5, they are his own and dear to him, and he keeps them as the apple of his eye, Psal. xvii. 8. He is round about them from henceforth and forever, as the mountains are round about Jerusalem, Psal. cxxv. 2. He protects their habitations as he did the tents of Israel in the wilderness, for he hath promised to create upon every dwelling place of mount Zion, a pillar of cloud by day, to shelter from heat; and the shining of a flaming fire by night, to shelter from cold, Isa. iv. 5. Thus he blesseth the habitations of the just, so that no real evil shall befall it, nor any plague come nigh it.

This care of the divine providence concerning us and our families, we are to depend upon, so as to look upon no provisions we make for our own safety sufficient, without the blessing of the divine providence upon it; except the

Lord keep the city, the watchman waketh but in vain. Be the house never so well built, the doors and windows never so well barred, the servants never so careful, never so watchful, it is all to no purpose, unless he that keeps Israel, and neither slumbers nor sleeps, undertakes for our safety; and if he be thy protector, at destruction and famine thou shalt laugh, and shalt know that thy tabernacle is in peace, Job v. 22, 24.

2. It is by the power of God's grace that we are enabled to think ourselves safe, and on that grace we must continually depend. The fear of danger, though groundless, is as vexatious as if it were never so just. And therefore to complete the mercy of being made to dwell safely, it is requisite that by the grace of God we be delivered from our fears, Psal. xxxiv. 4, as well as from the things themselves that we are afraid of; that shadows may not be a terror to us, no more than substantial evils.

If by the grace of God we are enabled to keep conscience void of offence, and still to preserve our integrity; if iniquity be put far away, and no wickedness suffered to dwell in our tabernacles; then shall we lift up our faces without spot, we shall be steadfast, and shall not need to fear, Job xi. 14, 15, for fear came in with sin, and goes out with it. If our hearts condemn us not, then have we confidence towards God, and man too, and are made to dwell securely, for we are sure nothing can hurt us but sin ; and whatever doth harm us, sin is the sting of it ; and therefore if sin be pardoned and prevented, we need not fear any trouble.

If by the grace of God we be enabled to live by faith, that faith which sets God always before us, that faith which applies the promises to ourselves, and puts them in suit at the throne of grace, that faith which purifies the heart, overcomes the world, and quenches all the fiery darts of the wicked one, that faith which realizeth unseen things, and is the substance and evidence of them : If we be acted and governed by his grace, we are made to dwell safely, and to bid defiance to death itself, and all its harbingers and terrors : O death where is thy sting ? This faith will not only silence our fears, but will open our lips in holy triumphs, if God be for us, who can be against us ?

Let us lie down in peace and sleep, not in the strength of a natural resolution against fear, nor merely of rational arguments against it, though they are of good use, but in a dependence upon the grace of God to work faith in us, and to fulfil in us the work of faith. This is going to sleep like a Christian, under the shadow of God's wings, going to sleep in faith ; and it will be to us a good earnest of dying in faith; for the same faith that will carry us cheerfully through the short death of sleep, will carry us through the long sleep of death.

For Application

First, See how much it is our concern to carry our religion about with us wherever we go, and to have it always at our right hand ; for at every turn we have occasion for it, lying down, rising up, going out, coming in ; and those that are Christians indeed, who confine not their religion to the new moons and the sabbaths, but bring the influences of it into all the common actions and occurrences of human life. We must sit down at our tables and rise from them, lie down in our beds, and arise from them, with an eye to God's providence and promise. Thus we must live a life of communion with God, even while our conversation is with the world.

And in order to this, it is necessary that we have a living principle in our hearts, a principle of grace, which like a well of living water, may be continually springing up to life eternal. John iv. 14. It is necessary likewise that we have a watchful eye upon our hearts, and keep them with all diligence, that we set a strict guard upon their motions, and have our thoughts more at command than I fear most Christians

have. See what need we have of the constant
supplies of divine grace, and of a union with
Christ, that by faith we may partake of the
root and fatness of the goodly olive continually.

Secondly, See what a hidden life the life of
good Christians is, and how much it lies from
under the eye and observation of the world.
The most important part of their business lies
between God and their own souls, in the frame
of their spirits, and the working of their hearts
in their retirements, which no eye sees but his
that is all eye. Justly are the saints called
God's hidden ones, and his secret is said to be
with them, for they have meat to eat, and
work to do which the world knows not of; and
joys, and griefs, and cares which a stranger
doth not intermeddle with. Great is the mystery of serious godliness.

And this is a good reason, why we should
look upon ourselves as incompetent judges one
of another, because we know not others' hearts,
nor are witnesses to their retirements. It is to
be feared, there are many whose religion lies
all in the outside, they make a fair show in
the flesh, and perhaps a great noise; and yet
are strangers to this secret communion with
God, in which consists so much of the power
of godliness. And on the other hand, it is to
be hoped, there are many who do not distin-

guish themselves by anything observable in
their profession of religion, but pass through
the world without being taken notice of, and
yet converse much with God in solitude, and
walk with him in the even constant tenor of a
regular devotion and conversation. The kingdom of God comes not with observation. Many
merchants thrive by a secret trade, that make
no bustle in the world. It is fit, therefore, that
every man's judgment should proceed from the
Lord, who knows men's hearts, and sees in
secret.

Thirdly, See what enemies they are to
themselves, that continue under the power of
a vain and carnal mind, and live without God
in the world. Multitudes I fear there are, to
whom all that has been said of secret communion with God is accounted as a strange thing,
and they are ready to say of their ministers
when they speak of it, do they speak parables?
They lie down and rise up, go out and come
in, in the constant pursuit either of worldly
profits, or of sensual pleasures : But God is not
in all their thoughts, not in any of them :
they live upon him, and upon the gifts of his
bounty from day to day, but they have no regard to him, never own their dependence on
him, nor are in any care to secure his favors.

They that live such a mere animal life as
this, do not only put a great contempt upon

God, but do a great deal of damage to themselves; they stand in their own light, and deprive themselves of the most valuable comforts that can be enjoyed on this side heaven. What peace can they have who are not at peace with God? What satisfaction can they take in their hopes, who build them not upon God the everlasting foundation? Or in their joys, who derive them not from him the fountain of life and living waters? O that at length they would be wise for themselves, and remember their Creator and Benefactor.

Fourthly, See what easy pleasant lives the people of God might live, if it were not their own faults. There are those who fear God and work righteousness, and are accepted of the Lord, but go drooping and disconsolate from day to day, are full of cares and fears, and complaints, and make themselves always uneasy; and it is because they do not live that life of delight in God and dependence on him, that they might and should live. God has effectually provided for their dwelling at ease, but they make not use of that provision he has laid up for them.

O that all who appear to be conscientious, and are afraid of sin, would appear to be cheerful, and afraid of nothing else; that all who call God Father, and are in care to please him, and keep themselves in his love, would learn to cast all their other care upon him, and commit their way to him as to a Father. He shall choose our inheritance for us, and knows what is best for us, better than we do for ourselves. Thou shalt answer, Lord, for me. It is what I have often said, and will abide by. That a holy heavenly life spent in the service of God, and in communion with him, is the most pleasant comfortable life anybody can live in this world.

Fifthly, See in this, what is the best preparation we can make for the changes, that may be before us in our present state ; and that is, to keep up a constant acquaintance and communion with God, to converse with him daily, and keep up stated times for calling on him, that so when trouble comes it may find the wheels of prayer a going. And then may we come to God with a humble boldness and comfort, and hope to speed when we are in affliction, if we have been no strangers to God at other times, but in our peace and prosperity had our eyes ever towards him.

Even when we arrive to the greatest degree of holy security and serenity, and lie down most in peace, yet still we must keep up an expectation of trouble in the flesh ; our ease must be grounded not upon any stability in the creature ; if it be, we put a cheat upon ourselves, and treasure up so much the greater vexation for ourselves. No, it must be built upon the faithfulness of God, which is unchangeable. Our Master has told us, in the world you shall have tribulation, much tribulation, count upon it, it is only in me that you shall have peace. But if every day be to us, as it should be, a sabbath of rest in God, and communion with him, nothing can come amiss to us any day, be it never so cross.

Sixthly, See in this, what is the best preparation we can make for the unchangeable world, that is before us. We know God will bring us to death, and it is our great concern to get ready for it. It ought to be the business of every day to prepare for our last day, and what can we do better for ourselves in the prospect of death, than by frequent retirements for communion with God, to get more loose from that world which at death we must leave, and better acquainted with that world which at death we must remove to. By going to our beds as to our graves, we shall make death familiar to us, and it will become as easy to us to close our eyes in peace and die, as it used to be to close our eyes in peace and sleep.

We hope God will bring us to heaven; and by keeping up daily communion with God, we grow more and more meet to partake of that inheritance; and have our conversation in heaven. It is certain, all that will go to heaven

hereafter begin their heaven now, and have
their hearts there ; if we thus enter into a spiritual rest every night, that will be a pledge of
our blessed repose in the embraces of divine
love, in that world wherein day and night
come to an end, and we shall not rest day or
night from praising him, who is, and will be,
our eternal rest.